Praise for *The Roadmap Home:*

Your GPS to Inner Peace

"I heartily endorse *The Roadmap Home* to the seeker of 'a better way.' "

> – Karen Casey, best-selling author of *Each Day a New Beginning*, www.womens-spirituality.com.

"The *Roadmap Home* offers us hope. Leonard Szymczak provides an honest portrayal of his personal life and demonstrates that hardships can offer blessings in disguise. He provides a map to help us connect with the Guiding Power of Spirit so we can find our way Home."

> – Gerald G Jampolsky, M.D., author of *Love is Letting Go of Fear*

"Where is Dorothy going in the Wizard of Oz? Where is Pilgrim going in Pilgrim's Progress? The last line of the original Star War's Trilogy is 'Let's go home.' Home is where the heart is. We are always headed home. Thank you Leonard for providing us with such a steady compass and a clear Roadmap Home."

> – Jon Mundy, Ph.D., lecturer and author of *What Is Mysticism?*

"I have been forever impacted by the beautiful stories, exercises and experiences that Leonard so wonderfully presents in his newest book. It is a powerful extension of the man himself. He answers the questions of who we are, where we come from, where we are going, and how we get there. By sharing his own personal story, Leonard immediately resonates with the reader, assuring them that we are all on a journey together."

> – Harry Tucker, strategy advisor and author in *97 Things Every Project Manager Should Know: Collective Wisdom from the Experts*

"A journey home requires a guide who has both been lost and found, a guide who is gentle in approach but frank and confident in offering direction. Leonard Szymczak is just such a guide. Many books are more of a walk around the block, providing hope but only returning us to where we began. The book you are holding in your hand is different, it can authentically make a true difference in your life by bringing you to feel, perhaps for the first time, at home within yourself."

> – Dr. Lee Jampolsky, author of *Smile for No Good Reason* and *Healing the Addictive Personality*

"Finding peace in our lives can often seem as difficult as setting a VCR. But, when you realize that you have your own GPS to do just that, you can relax and enjoy the ride. In his book, Leonard Szymczak shares his personal journey of finding that GPS and offers practical ways that you can find it too. Through guided exercises he helps you to set and follow your own GPS to inner peace."

> – Beverly Hutchinson McNeff, editor of *The Holy Encounter* magazine

"I have a deep love and respect for Leonard and know that his integrity and commitment will transform people's lives. He has a contagious enthusiasm and a dedicated intention to help people. *The Roadmap Home* will touch people's lives and show them how to achieve a deep sense of inner peace."

> – Rev. Sandy Moore, Center for Spiritual Living Orange County, author of *Green Intentions: Creating a Spiritual Foundation for a Green Lifestyle.*

"Leonard is an amazing spirit and his gift of communicating a deep understanding of our essence and how we interact with our world is a blessing to us all. This book is transformational!"

> – Rev. Kirk Moore, Center for Spiritual Living Orange County, author of *Tara's Angels.*

LEONARD SZYMCZAK

THE ROADMAP HOME

Your GPS to Inner Peace

ISBN: 1-4392-5126-6
ISBN-13: 9781439251263
LCCN: 2009907522

GPS cover concept: Marilyn Reilly
Back cover photograph: Bill Motlong

1. Self-help. 2. Personal growth. 3. Spiritual

Visit www.booksurge.com to order additional copies.

To my mother, Estelle Szymczak, who demonstrated, time and time again, the meaning of sacrifice and perseverance as she overcame adversity to provide a home for her family.

To my sisters, Marilyn and Rita, and my brother Jim, who drew upon heroic qualities as they courageously scaled their own difficult mountains.

To my children, Melissa and Nate, who blessed me with their loving spirits and taught me about the meaning of home.

TABLE OF CONTENTS

ACKNOWLEDGEMENTS

Writing is a solitary process. However, completing a book involves a community. There have been countless people who have supplied help, offered suggestions, provided loving support, and inspired my writing odyssey. It would take a chapter to fully recognize all those who contributed to this book. Clearly, the courageous stories that my clients shared with me had an enormous impact on my own life and for that, I am forever grateful.

I want to recognize and offer my heartfelt thanks to my Home Team:

Marilyn Reilly, for her tremendous support, suggestions and cover concepts; and her husband, Bob, for his good-humored input.

Nate Szymczak, the graphic wizard, for his encouraging words, computer help, and gifted vision in transforming concepts into images.

Rita Szymczak, for enthusiastically cheering me up the mountain, offering wonderful advice, and creating tables.

Melissa Szymczak, for her practical advice to keep my feet firmly planted on the ground.

Bill Motlong, for being my sounding board, honest reviewer, creative consultant, longtime friend, and personal photographer.

Suzie Trisler, for her sound advice and cheerleading.

Mary Harris, for her generosity of spirit as well as her wordsmithing.

Janae Stewart, for her astute editing and assistance.

Gary Dukarich, for reviewing the manuscript with the keen eyes of a hawk.

Irene Vincent, for creatively expressing the initial design.

Stephanie Lloyd and Reverend Pamela Murphy, for their ongoing intentional support.

Lisa Nichols, author of *No Matter What*, for suggesting the format of teleseminars to review chapters of the manuscript.

Those who regularly attended the teleseminars and offered feedback and encouragement, chapter by chapter, to prod me up the publishing mountain: Diane Coutre, Alexandra Kaplan, Bonnie Lewis, Chuck Miller, Jesi Silveria, Richard Smith, and Harry Tucker. The annotated pages of corrections by Harry and Richard provided gold nuggets of advice. Thank you.

Those who stopped in, every now and then, for the teleseminars and contributed ideas and encouragement.

Those who attended The Roadmap Home Seminars, for helping me refine the concepts so they were more easily understood.

Those others who, in their own unique and special way, contributed to the process of birthing the manuscript: Grace Avalon, Brad Axelrad, Danna Beal, Jeannine Caryl, Robin Condro, April Durrett, Don Hobbs, Jonathan Morgan Jenkins, Audrey Jones, Diana Kenny, Marcus, Charlene Michel, Barbara Motlong, D'Marie Mulattieri, Susan Robertson, Michelle Morris Spieker, Elaine Stahlhofen, Robana Stevenson, Leti Stiles, Barbara Sunday, Sarah Sutton, Theresa Swift, and Diane Wisner. Thank you all.

I also wish to acknowledge those whose shining light helped to illuminate my own path: Reverends Sandi and Kirk Moore and the Center for Spiritual Living Orange County; CEO Space; Chicago South Suburban Men's group; A Course in Miracles Study Group; Dahn Yoga Center; The Law of Attraction Center Orange County; Light Bearers of the World; Miracle Distribution Center; and Toastmasters of Dana Point.

And finally, to the many others who encouraged me up the mountain, I offer my deepest gratitude. Your helping hands made the climb toward publication less arduous and more joyful.

INTRODUCTION

Everyone's life is a story. Within each story there's an amazing journey. That journey comes with a narrative – how we describe the journey and the meaning we give each experience. That narrative provides a framework that shapes the way we view the past, live the present, and perceive the future. It's a roadmap that sets our course and highlights lessons. Roadmaps and stories, however, do change. Since this book is about change and transformation, it seems fitting that I start with my personal journey.

The first time my father left the family I was six. The second time was for good and I was nine. My mother worked in a factory on the south side of Chicago and with four children to feed, her hands were full. Too full to clean, cook, work and tend children. Too full to cradle a frightened child or whisper, "I love you" to a broken heart.

Out of desperation, she considered a heart other than her own to pump life into her children. She took my brother, two sisters and me to visit Mooseheart, a residential childcare facility outside Chicago. Her intention was clear. If she couldn't care for us, she would explore an alternative.

Even if a moose had a heart attached to its name, I knew it was an orphanage. It wasn't an awful facility but it was a disturbing venue for a Sunday excursion in the summer of '57. When we toured the grounds, I didn't get mad, sad or act bad, even though I was faced with the prospect of leaving the familiar to live in a frightening new place with a group of strangers. I was ready to accept the decision, for I had learned to adapt and accommodate – keys to survival. At that tender age of nine, I didn't need an orphanage to realize I had lost my home.

Home is about belonging – to a place, a group of people, a wellspring of love. A place where one is comforted, nurtured and protected. Where one can feel safe and secure and can gather strength in the face of adversity. Most importantly, it's a place to live one's truth.

That was not my home. Mine was a place ravaged by my father's mental illness, domestic violence, blaming parents, and their impending divorce. It was a place riddled with conflict, fear and anxiety. Home was not a fortress of protection. Rather, it was a crumbling castle with dragons spewing hot flames. I felt insecure and unsafe, and realized later that I had lost a more sacred space – that place of inner knowing where I had inalienable rights – the right to exist, to feel, to think and act, to love and be loved, to express myself and be heard, to see my potential and have it recognized and blessed. That home was clearly lost by the time I visited the orphanage.

To survive my childhood I learned to shut down. I forgot about that inner knowing and replaced it with voices of anxiety and fear. Becoming orphaned from my sacred truth was the harshest of losses. To manage the fear, grief, anger and shame simmering underneath, I adopted defenses – silence, avoidance, and suppression, along with a dash of sarcasm and dark humor. I had learned that life was not about love, it was purely survival.

Fortunately, there were slivers of hope. My three siblings as fellow orphans offered some companionship and comfort. As well, my Polish grandmother helped soothe my soul. Her English was poor so I couldn't talk about problems, yet she acted as a haven in an ugly firestorm. With her support my mother, thankfully, made the courageous decision to rear her children for better and for worse.

Though we never moved to that place with the heart of a moose, my anxiety and fear remained. It turned into a faint hum coursing through my veins like electricity, urging me to be alert, ever ready, on edge, because home as I knew it could be stolen in a flash.

I never talked about the humming and carried on as if nothing was wrong. During times of uncertainty and insecurity, the hum would vibrate more intensely, forcing me to be vigilant about any possible threat. I often ignored the hum and followed my mother's dictum, "Get busy and forget your problems."

It wasn't until after I became a psychotherapist that I realized the damage caused by neglect, abuse and abandonment. Deeper insidious wounds resulted from the ways I adapted and accommodated. No talking, no feeling, no crying, no sign of a whimper – even when my heart was humming with pain. Denial and disconnection were not the best ways to manage wounds, yet without much guidance or direction it was hard to act otherwise.

Nonetheless, out of our deepest wounds come our greatest gifts. The amazing gift I received from my childhood was a quest. And that quest was to find home.

My quest led me to a Catholic seminary where I attended high school and college. I needed a "father" and what better place to find one than in the priesthood? My quest, however, eventually guided me away from organized religion into the field of social work and family therapy. I could easily relate to families whose broken homes were fraught with conflict and despair and needed healing and repair.

My quest led me to love and marriage and to Australia where my two children were born. After 14 years Down Under, my family returned to Chicago where I faced many potholes and detours. After 26 years of marriage, I went through a difficult divorce in 1996. That period rocked my foundation. But out of the rubble, I began to hear the cry of the orphan.

I discovered that the inner Home, though buried, had not been extinguished. The heartbeat pulsed with a rhythm of life. The sound was often faint, but the message was clear – return to the place of inner knowing. Wake-up calls shook me from my unconscious state. Those bolts of lightning sent tremors rippling through my psyche. The widening fissures in my defense system allowed me to turn my eyes inward past the ruins of old preconceptions and toward the beckoning heart of authentic connection.

Finding the way back required courage and dedication. It demanded a willingness to recognize the calls, liberate the orphan and awaken from a numbed existence. I had to share stories, release tears, and embrace forgiveness. The healing energy of acceptance and love provided soothing balm for the orphan's heart.

My quest has brought me to Southern California. I realize, however, that Home is not the result of finding a place, living with a person, establishing a career, or having material success. Rather, Home resides in the heart and soul and remains with us wherever we go. Home is anywhere and everywhere.

Though we may journey through the shadow of death or climb majestic mountains, we are never orphaned as long as we remain connected to the Guiding Power of Spirit. That connection endows us with wonderful gifts – to delight in the senses, to experience emotions and feel joy, to exercise our free will, to love and be loved, to express ourselves, to see our true potential and satisfy our dreams. We are never alone but rather interconnected with others in the Oneness of Being.

During my 35-plus years as a therapist and educator, as well as decades of personal growth, I have witnessed in myself and with others thousands of wake-up calls. Some took the form of marital disharmony or divorce, depression or anxiety, debilitating addictions, physical illnesses, financial losses or traumatic accidents. Those who failed to "see the light" were destined to slide back into the dark hole of unconsciousness and sleepwalk, unaware of their true potential. Nevertheless, calls unanswered persist and intensify. Old patterns need to be broken and new habits forged so that vision can be restored.

Once awakened to a heightened state of awareness, we can distinguish the stark contrast between limited living and consciously being. Our internal GPS, the Guiding Power of Spirit, beckons us back to our True Self. This may provoke both exhilaration and fear. Exhilaration about returning Home; fear about the shifting ground beneath long-held beliefs. Though we may cling to a familiar false self, the Guiding Power of Spirit always emits a homing beacon to show the way.

I offer myself as a guide to your self-discovery and invite you as the hero/heroine of your unfolding story to step through a threshold and embrace the quest for your True Self. My heartfelt wish is that you open your mind and heart, connect with your GPS, and return Home to inner peace.

OVERVIEW

Taking a journey into the unknown with a map in

hand fills me with anticipation.

– Michael White

The Global Positioning System is a worldwide navigational system that determines exact locations. When a receiver is activated in a car, it detects its current position, processes the requested destination, produces a map, and charts a precise course. We can then comfortably cruise along the highway without much worry. What we often don't realize, however, is that we have an internal GPS that does exactly the same thing. Our GPS, Guiding Power of Spirit, always knows where we are and steers us along life's highways toward our ultimate destination – Home. (I capitalize "Home" whenever I refer to that sacred place where we are connected with Spirit.)

Home is a place beyond the ego's identity. It's the realization that we are connected with an infinite Source of Wisdom that beckons us to love and inner peace. Regrettably, we often rush through life with little concern or awareness of this guiding system. When we lose that connection, we perceive home as outside ourselves and construct an identity and psychological defenses to protect a "false self" – a composite of beliefs downloaded from caregivers, culture and society. Our "false self" seeks material possessions, relationships and experiences to provide happiness and inner peace. We then wander aimlessly like orphans, without a roadmap, unplugged from our GPS.

This book maps a route to connect with our ever-present navigational system. That route takes us through the stages of spiritual awakening. Since all living beings evolve through phases of development, it stands to reason that spiritual development operates under similar principles. After all, we transition through birth, childhood, adolescence, adulthood and finally, old age and death unless we die prematurely. Each stage follows a blueprint and is necessary for the succeeding phases. A teenager raised in New York City will have a different experience of adolescence than an Amish boy growing up in Pennsylvania. Nevertheless, both will undergo puberty. Family and culture merely define what is and isn't acceptable. The same applies toward our spiritual journey.

Though we are always connected to an infinite Source, the awakening process is about shifting from one phase to the next. Some of us may be unconscious infants, oblivious to Spirit, while others are maturing into spiritual adults who feel more connected to a Divine Presence. Religious experiences and rituals may color the process, but transformation occurs as we develop through spiritual levels, regardless of religious preferences.

Consider the caterpillar. Though the butterfly receives the glory as the universal symbol of transformation, we often diminish the lowly caterpillar as far less attractive. This wiggling earthbound creature with a voracious appetite hungrily consumes leaf after leaf before it experiences a metamorphosis. It evolves naturally and perfectly through phases until it spins a cocoon in preparation for flight. Without the caterpillar, there is no butterfly.

Like caterpillars, some of us are emerging from tiny eggs while others are consuming life experiences and shedding old beliefs. Some are entering dark cocoons and others are preparing to flutter skyward. We may be at different phases but we are all, nonetheless, climbing that mountain toward freedom and a connection to All That Is.

Once we recognize that we are in process, we can rest assured that our GPS will direct us along the awakening path. Each of us follows a unique course with individualized lessons. Some of us may need to be hit by a bolt of lightning, like Paul on the road to Damascus. Others may respond to gentle reminders. It's only a matter of time before we realize our true nature and emerge from the cocoon.

The process of our evolving spiritual development is depicted in the diagram of a flower with six petals. Each petal represents a stage of development: Adaptation; Becoming an Orphan; Wake-up Calls and Signposts; Staying Awake; Healing Wounds and

Breaking Free; and Heartbeat of Connection. They lead us Home to the center of the flower which represents the beginning and the end, the alpha and the omega, the very core of our being, our True Self.

To appreciate the awakening process, imagine a long day of adapting to the countless demands of the world. We fall fast asleep and enter dreamland. The dreams, however, seem so real that we soon believe they are reality. We wander like orphans, lost from Home. Our internal GPS sets off an alarm, a reminder that we are having a depressing dream. We may ignore the wake-up call and bury ourselves under the covers. After persistent prodding and flashing neon signs, we eventually answer the call. Thus begins our awakening.

We are initially reluctant to climb out of our comfortable bed of beliefs but, in order to break free of the paralyzing dream, we must let go of our fears and heal our minds. With ongoing practice we strengthen the heartbeat of connection so we can return Home and experience sublime moments of inner peace and Oneness. However, the material world intrudes once again and we fall back to sleep ready to repeat the cycle.

In our spiritual development we spiral around the circle, moving steadily inward from one petal to the next. This evolving journey expands our consciousness and steadily increases our ability to stay awake. As we spiral inward, we extend our light outward. We radiate our consciousness to the outside world which mirrors it back to us. This allows us to see ourselves more clearly. The cycle shifts us to deeper levels of consciousness as we release limitations.

Like the caterpillar, our transformational journey ultimately causes a metamorphosis wherein we experience ourselves more fully as spiritual beings on a human excursion. From our center, we're inspired to serve our highest good and interact with the world in a loving, purposeful way. We understand that our GPS is always with us while we travel the winding road with its challenging detours, hidden tunnels, exhilarating climbs, and wonderful miracles.

Let's briefly preview each leg of the journey.

Chapter One discusses the **MEANING OF HOME,** our original bliss. We understand that we can experience an ongoing connection with the Guiding Power of Spirit. From this awakened perspective, we can feel at home with six vehicles that may be referred to as instruments or petals of our flowering life:

1) An evolving sensory physical body that interacts with the external world
2) A range of emotions that provides feedback about our internal world
3) An inquisitive mind that processes information and directs attention
4) An open heart that relates with love and compassion
5) A voice that freely expresses our inner truth
6) A vision that sees through illusion and recognizes talents and a divine purpose

In Chapter Two, **ADAPTATION**, we explore our descent into the material world. Once we are born, we download files and programs, some of which contain viruses from our parents, culture and society. We construct an identity comprised of these beliefs and adopt roles and behavioral patterns. Over time, this "false self" becomes attached to the transitory world of material possessions and relationships and begins to forget about Home. This creates separation which leads to insecurity, anxiety and fear.

Chapter Three, **BECOMING AN ORPHAN,** highlights the period when we fall asleep at the wheel and lose the connection with our GPS. An orphan is someone who is furthest away from Home. At the same time, an orphan stops being "at home" in the body, emotions, mind, heart, voice and vision. Orphans sleepwalk through life, unconscious about behavioral patterns, the interconnection of life, and the myriad of choices available. Unaware of the internal navigational system, an orphan wanders aimlessly and perceives life from the vantage point of a victim, resigned to an unhappy, and sometimes dramatic, life of desperation. Homelessness, however, creates longing for connection.

In Chapter Four, **WAKE-UP CALLS AND SIGNPOSTS**, we discover that loving whispers beckon our awakening. When we don't respond, our True Self employs a principle of thermodynamics to crack open our unconscious mind. Intense heat generated by traumas and personal crises produces transformation so eyes can turn inward toward authentic connection.

If we answer the call, signposts appear to assist us through the dense fog. They show up when we least expect and may serendipitously appear in relationships, words, music, symbols, animals, nature or dreams.

Chapter Five, **STAYING AWAKE**, asks us to leave familiar terrain and enter the tunnel of transformation. This transition stage is often marked by confusion, terror and anxiety as we face the fear of losing our identity and cherished beliefs. Since an awakened state heightens awareness, we may feel worse as painful memories, long suppressed, are brought to light. Once we make the declaration to return Home, there's no turning back.

Now we are ready to engage the Guiding Power of Spirit. With our internal gyroscope we distinguish between life choices that create discord and those that resonate with our True Self. We learn to pay attention to each holy instant by using a simple process:

Observe, Accept, Forgive, Ask, Listen and *Receive.* We begin to recognize incredible opportunities in every moment.

In Chapter Six, **HEALING WOUNDS AND BREAKING FREE**, we release ourselves from a numbed existence and shift destructive thoughts, feelings, and behaviors. We learn to apply the IR-SPEA anti-virus program, whereby we: *Inspect* our beliefs and life patterns; *Reject* and release outmoded thoughts and painful emotions; *Select* healing, loving beliefs congruent with our True Self; *Project* these new beliefs into the world with conscious intention; *Expect* wonderful encounters and miraculous results; and *Accept* deepening love and tranquility.

Chapter Seven, **HEARTBEAT OF CONNECTION**, expands the powerful principles of *Love, Trust* and *Self-mastery,* and teaches us to consciously fine-tune the six instruments of body, emotions, mind, heart, voice and vision so we can play in concert with Spirit. With training and focus, we become more attuned to the Home channel and expand our heart and clarify our life's purpose.

In Chapter Eight, **CONSCIOUS CREATION,** we focus on the art of co-creating from the inside out with Spirit rather than from ego. We use our well-tuned instruments to play at a higher frequency and move through the stages of conscious creation, whereby we: *Identify Needs; Clarify Intentions; State Intentions; Know and Create; Review Roadblocks*; and *Allow and Be Grateful.* Intentions that resonate with our GPS seek the highest good and vibrate with love.

Chapter Nine, **HOMECOMING: INNER PEACE**, takes us into the realm of innocent children who delight in being. We welcome *Celebration, Childlike Innocence, Abundance, Faith, Inner Peace* and a *Home Team.* We open up the throttle and roar with inspiration. We celebrate the gifts of each day, feel the wellspring of love, live a life of purpose, create loving supports and embrace the Guiding Power of Spirit. We view setbacks as lessons to practice love and forgiveness and, with raised consciousness, we experience moments of Oneness – Home.

Following each chapter, I include a mapping exercise and a guided visualization and suggest you work with a journal. It provides a sacred space and place to record your awakening process and strengthen your inward connection.

I have utilized the tools of journaling and visualization over the past 35 years. Journals expanded my awareness as I documented my dreams, aspirations, life patterns, inadequacies, emotional states, self-defeating behaviors, relationships, wake-up calls, visions, victories and mystical experiences. Visualizations brought incredible gifts of insight, healing and direction. I encourage you to make use of these valuable processes.

One further thought. Some mapping exercises and visualizations may trigger emotional responses and raise childhood memories. You may experience a wave of anxiety or sadness, or confusing physical sensations such as tightness in the throat or chest. You may also become acutely aware of your patterns with significant relationships. Therefore, consider establishing a supportive network of people who can act as resources. This may involve a friend, partner, support group, therapist or other individuals who can assist you on your journey.

When you travel in a group or with a companion, road trips can be very rewarding. Therefore, select those who can create a non-judgmental, safe environment that encourages openness, support and individual space to connect with your True Self.

You're now ready to move through any roadblocks toward the beckoning heart of authentic connection. With your trustworthy GPS and this easy-to-follow roadmap, be prepared for a transformational adventure where problems and pain become opportunities for personal growth, forgiveness and love. Wipe the sleep from your eyes and open the map. Activate the receiver and set the course.

It's time to return Home to inner peace.

CHAPTER ONE

MEANING OF HOME

Be grateful for the home you have, knowing that

at this moment, all you have is all you need.

– Sarah Ban Breathnach

"According to a Hindu legend, humans had so abused their divine powers that the gods decided to remove their divinity and hide it where men would never find it. . . . The wisest of the gods said, 'We will hide it deep within man himself, for that is the last place he would ever think to look for it.' "[1]

We are in an age where more people are actively searching within for spirituality. The visionary Jean Houston tells us that we are evolving from *homo sapiens* into *homo spiritualis.* This growing realization that we are spiritual beings having a human excursion means that we are returning to the center of our being – our true Home.

The word "home" conjures up images of our birthplace. We often think of belonging to a wellspring of love where we feel safe and secure and gather strength in the face of adversity. Our inner Home is where innocence, joy, love and peace are natural states. It is a holy sanctuary of rest and comfort. It is a Garden of Eden – paradise linked to an Infinite, All-Knowing Source. The destination is already programmed, for we are, in fact, already Home. If we return to our center, we would realize Home is always with us.

If our experience growing up was traumatic, we may react to the concept of home with revulsion. Our ego will tell us to stay away from home because we will only get hurt. That was my experience growing up. In the summertime I was usually the last kid on the block to return indoors after spending the day outside. My mother was often asleep on the couch after a long day working in the factory, followed by a list of chores to care for the family. I didn't feel particularly welcomed or desired. That seemed normal to me. I knew my mother had plenty on her plate.

When I studied psychology and social work, my perception changed. I began to question the meaning of home. Over many years, I have come to realize that the real Home is our connection with Spirit or whatever name you wish to use – Creative Intelligence, All That Is, Higher Power, Source, the Force, the Divine or God. Whatever the name or concept, suffice it to say that Spirit pulsates through us and our world. As Ernest Holmes wrote, "There is a living Spirit at the center of your being. The original Author of all life is in and around you."[2]

Our Home is a place of incredible inner peace where love is our natural state. Love goes beyond ego, without guilt or shame. Love is joyful and unconditional and has nothing to do with performance or behavior. It simply is, without limits, boundaries or expectations. True love encompasses all that we are.

The universal story is about returning back Home to that place of love and peace. Our minds and thoughts have created a veil of illusion that prevents us from embracing that world. Yet we all yearn to return.

The Wizard of Oz epitomizes our quest. By the end of her journey, Dorothy realized there was no place like home. The ultimate quest is to muster the courage to bring our minds and hearts back to that inner knowing.

When we're Home, we perceive each moment as an opportunity for growth. We have what the Buddhists call a "beginner's mind." Unattached to outcomes, we see every encounter as a holy lesson. With a stillness of mind, we step into Oneness.

To return to that Oneness, we need a navigational system. The Guiding Power of Spirit is, in effect, our internal GPS. It permeates all areas of our lives and charts the course to our ultimate destination. We may not understand the lessons along the way, but our individual routes offer all that we need. Faith allows us to comfortably cruise on life's superhighway without worry. However, we must activate our receiver and tune in to the Guiding Power of Spirit.

Before proceeding, let's clear up a few misconceptions. Religion often promotes a dualistic approach about body and soul, heaven and earth. This concept separates the physical from the spiritual and creates the appearance that only in death can souls be liberated and experience heaven.

Thomas Aquinas described the soul as the ultimate intrinsic source of vital living activity. The word intrinsic suggests that it is basic, inherent and essential. James Thornton, in *A Field Guide to the Soul*, described the soul as "Already fully awakened, perfect, always sustained, unborn, and undying. It knows the sacred in everything."[3] It is our True Self.

The soul is intrinsically connected with the divine and expands outward through six vehicles – body, emotions, mind, heart, voice and vision – that create a matrix of interactions and interconnections in the community and with the environment. Spirit pulsates through us continually and extends outward to others.

We may not experience this continual flow because our vehicles often stall in stressful, dark tunnels, thereby affecting our ability to receive the signal and be conscious of our GPS. Think of our cell phones. We may periodically lose the connection when we enter a 'dead zone'; then we ask, "Can you hear me now?" In reality, Spirit's signal is ever-present. We merely have to move out of our defensive tunnels to get better reception.

This requires that we cycle through stages of spiritual growth. As we travel through each cycle, we move deeper within to that place where heaven and earth are one. From this perspective, we are meant to be at home with six vehicles: an evolving sensory physical body that interacts with the external world; a range of emotions that provides feedback about our internal world; an inquisitive mind that processes information and directs attention; an open heart that relates with love and compassion; a voice that freely expresses our inner truth; and a vision that sees past illusion and recognizes our divine purpose.

When we're at home with both the internal and external worlds, we can experience Oneness merely by walking along the beach, talking with a close friend or eating a sumptuous meal. With our body, emotions, mind, heart, voice and vision connected to Spirit we would know what we're meant to do, where we're meant to go, who we're supposed to talk to, why we're supposed to meet and what we're supposed to say. And it would flow easily and naturally.

If we do experience that depth of connection, it usually lasts for brief moments that become "holy instants." The reason has to do with our own evolution. After birth, we began to move away from our center and consume experiences like a voracious caterpillar. All this is a prerequisite for transformation. At the moment, our species is entering a grand awakening. Similar to the cicadas that, after years of hibernating underground, erupt en masse through the earth's crust, we are accelerating the return to our Source.

Returning to the center requires that we expand our concept of Home. Instead of thinking of our body or mind as separate from Spirit, we can recognize that Spirit permeates a flowering life. This is illustrated by a flower with six petals.

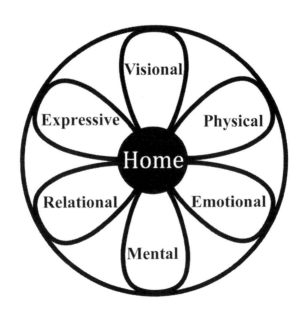

Spirit spirals outward into the physical, emotional, mental, relational, expressive and visional realms. (This process reflects elements of the Eastern system of chakras – energy vortexes in the body. For further information on chakras, see Dr. Anodea Judith in the bibliography.) Spirit shines the Home light into each petal, which then becomes a vehicle for awakening. Every petal can exhibit the light and take us inward toward Home.

Each petal is an essential aspect of our flowering creation. If we perceive them as separate from Spirit, we, in essence, pluck the petals off the flower. Of course, we can become so preoccupied with the petals that we forget the oneness of the flower. Therefore, we must learn to bring Spirit into the six realms of our lives and, at the same time, use them to establish a connection with Home.

Let's use a computer analogy. Imagine that Home represents a wireless connection to Spirit. We have the capacity to receive unlimited information from our GPS. The computer frame and motherboard symbolize the physical body while electricity or power represents emotions. The software programs and files signify the mind and the online social networks represent the realm of relationships. The speakers and keyboard symbolize expression while the screen becomes the symbol for vision. If we neglect or abuse the hardware, disconnect the power source, download viruses and dysfunctional programs, avoid social networks, turn off the sound, disable the keyboard and shut off the screen, we could never access the wireless connection. Every aspect of the computer is vital.

In a similar fashion, we need a body, feelings, mind, heart, voice and vision to receive and follow the direction of the Guiding Power of Spirit. The ego would have us believe that we are our bodies, feelings and thoughts, when in actuality, they are on loan, ours to use just like the computer with all its components. As we come to know each petal as a vehicle for our GPS, we realize that we have a sacred task to expand them. If any realm is shut down, such as our emotions, we limit the inflow and outflow. We don't want to detach the petals from the stem. Rather, we want to strengthen the connection with each petal. This increases our receptivity to the Guiding Power of Spirit.

Let's explore each petal.

Physical Home

Your body is your temple, or so I've heard it said. Is that because it houses our Being to which we each are wed? – Robana Stevenson

When we're connected to Home and travel in the vehicle of our body, we experience union, which is what the word "yoga" means. Consider the perfect union of a tiny baby floating safely in the uterus, symbiotically connected with the mother. The infant's needs are easily provided through the umbilical cord.

Once the baby is born, s/he learns to become a self-regulatory organism that relies on senses to register temperature, odor, taste, sound, touch and images. These senses provide critical feedback so the body can interact with the external world and establish union. Senses activate parts of the brain that register pleasure and pain. An infant smiles or coos when pampered and cries when distressed. His or her survival is dependent on the sensory input and response. When a child feels cold or hungry s/he reacts so the caregivers can respond.

Humans record experiences with a multitude of senses. We may remember a time when we snuggled against a parent, munched a yummy cookie, smelled a fragrant rose, watched a crawling cat-erpillar with wide-eyed curiosity, or sang a melody. The images, sounds, touches, tastes and smells of our childhood are stored in our memory banks. Our senses can lead us to experience life as heavenly if we had loving encounters or hellish if we endured hardship, trauma or suffering.

When we experience fear, the fight/flight response becomes activated. The survival instinct triggers the body to shut down peripheral systems such as the digestive tract and re-allocate resources to flee or prepare for battle. Living out of survival shuts down the connection to Home.

We can also sever the connection by flooding our lives with multi-sensory inputs. Consider the number of people rushing through life, multi-tasking on computers and cell phones while listening to music and wolfing a meal. Is it any wonder that we rely on medication to regulate our body?

Our body as an intricate working organism is truly incred-ible. The sympathetic and parasympathetic systems operate in the background to regulate temperature, circulate blood and oxygen, maintain our organs, regenerate cells, and more. And these processes occur without conscious attention. If there is a problem, the body sounds an alert. Hunger or thirst signals the brain for fuel or fluid. Our brain processes information so we can perceive, assess, evaluate and make decisions with incredible speed.

According to Ilchi Lee, founder of Brain respiration, "When we are sensitive and responsive to the signs and rhythms of our body, we are more deeply connected to the rich, wonderful texture of all life experience."[4] Not surprisingly, when we're connected with our body, we become better receptors for our GPS. Our eyes, ears, nose, taste buds and skin can recognize divine moments. We can soak in a sunset, listen to Mozart, smell freshly baked bread, savor a mango, and feel the warm embrace of a loved one. Without senses we couldn't feel the rapture of love.

Since the body is the temple of Spirit, we can refurbish the temple by making time for exercise and nutrition, rest and rejuvenation. We can pamper and strengthen the body with balance, not obsession. We can treat the body as an intelligent organism that talks to us daily and offers guidance. Should we have pain or a malady, we can listen to the body's messages to act in a way that guides us back Home.

Even if we were born with physical restrictions, we can still find Home. Helen Keller was deaf and blind, but she used other senses to connect with the Divine. Christopher Reeve was paralyzed from an equestrian accident yet said that some people with all their limbs were more paralyzed than he. In *Tuesdays with Morrie*, Mitch Abom wrote the incredible story of Morrie Schwartz who, though dying from Lou Gehrig's disease, remained connected to life while in a debilitating body until the very end.

No matter what condition the body is in, we can slowly move back into alignment with our physical form so that it becomes a vehicle to connect with and express Spirit. We can delight in the body, awaken our senses, connect with nature, and become both grounded and expansive. We can learn self-mastery tools such as conscious breathing and yoga to generate power and establish a bridge to the Divine.

This inventory offers you an opportunity to check in with your physical vehicle.

Physical Inventory

- Are you comfortable in your body?

- How do you take care of your body?

- What aspects of your physical self need attention, i.e. exercise, nutrition, rest, etc.?

- What gives you physical pleasure?

- Can you think of ways in which your body helps you connect with Spirit?

Emotional Home

God turns you from one feeling to another, and teaches by means of opposites, so that you have two wings to fly, not one. – Rumi

Our emotional home connects us with our internal world, propels energy into motion and teaches us about relationships and the environment. It becomes a vehicle for authentic expression. We're meant to experience a wide range of emotions and learn about expressing and managing them.

While we obviously want to feel joy and love more often than pain and grief, it's important to realize that all emotions, including sadness, fear and anger, play an important role. They help us identify needs, wants and desires and move us toward action. Discordant emotions alert us to problems and harmonious ones lead us to inner peace.

The interplay of opposites assists us to fly as suggested by Rumi's poem. Without fear we don't experience courage. Without sorrow, we don't fully embrace gratitude. Without anxiety or worry, we don't appreciate ease and contentment. The thought of losing a partner can heighten our desire to share love.

Each emotion, like a color on a painter's palette, offers contrast. An artist can utilize hues of reds, blues and yellows to create a richly textured picture. We are all artists and emotions are the colors on life's canvas.

Young children tend to express themselves freely. When upset, they cry and when happy, smile or laugh. Over time, they are conditioned to refrain from using certain colors. Boys are taught not to paint with tears; girls not to use anger. However, suppressed emotions stifle energy and creativity. Depression is repressed anger turned within. Any time we deny our feelings, we cause them to go underground where they ferment and expand until they find an alternative form of expression.

I learned this firsthand as a child. I suppressed truckloads of sadness and anger. Furthermore, I spent eight years in the seminary, not the best place to learn about sensuality or sexuality. When I was in my mid-20's, I knew I had to expand my box of emotional colors so I attended sensitivity groups which were quite popular in the seventies. They awakened my senses and helped me get in touch with feelings I never knew existed. It was as if I took the lid off a giant box of crayons that contained 96 colors, including gold and silver. I left the groups emotionally expanded and began to connect with others on a deeper level. With added colors to draw upon, I became more enthusiastic about life. Interestingly, "enthusiasm" comes from the Greek words *en* and *theos,* which mean "in God."

It must be said that being at home with our emotions doesn't mean we have license to infringe on others' rights. If we're angry, we can't just smack someone. Staying present in our emotions merely suggests that we acknowledge our feelings and process them. When we take time to review an emotion without judgment, we increase our self-understanding. We can learn to express feelings appropriately so that we move toward connection with others rather than away from them.

Most of us feel closer to a person after we share intimate feelings. And if we resolve conflict together, we're drawn even closer. Emotions are the glue in relationships. Therefore, it's important to stay present without shutting down feelings or moving toward excessive extremes.

When we're out of balance, Spirit uses our emotions to guide us back Home. We may be instructed to forgive when we feel angry, to love when we are frightened. As we move closer to Home, we nurture gratitude and joy. We recognize that emotions are a vehicle to extend love and forgiveness to others.

Take a moment to check in with your feelings.

Emotional Inventory

- Do you feel comfortable with your emotions?

- What emotions do you express or suppress? (joy, anger, love, sadness, happiness, fear, playfulness, guilt, pleasure)

- How do you satisfy your emotional needs?

- How often do you allow yourself to feel good and under what circumstances?

- Can you think of ways in which your emotions help you connect with Spirit?

Mental Home

Our life is what our thoughts make it. – Marcus Aurelius

We possess a beautifully inquisitive mind that processes information and directs our attention. Our mind is the vehicle that steers us through life. It provides focus, direction and willpower. Every day it processes thousands of thoughts like incoming text messages and makes countless decisions. Some thoughts receive immediate attention; others are filed away.

The power of our thoughts cannot be underestimated. We become what we think. The mind is a collection of interacting thoughts that create energy. It organizes information into structures and patterns in order to create stability or homeostasis. But the mind is not static. It also follows the principles of morphogenesis, meaning that it continually evolves and changes. It takes information, associates it with past experiences, evaluates the input, then decides on the best course of action – all at lightning speed.

The mind is both a sending and receiving station, much like a radio transmitter, and interconnects the internal and the external worlds. Emotionalized thoughts and beliefs act like positive and negative poles of a magnet. This is the law of attraction. We draw to us what we think. What we perceive mirrors our inner beliefs.

Awareness deepens our consciousness of our mental processes, which then furthers our personal choices. With attention and intention, we send out our thoughts on a "universal frequency" that allows us to connect with other minds. A collective consciousness creates the visible world. This is clearly mimicked by the worldwide web. However, there is also a collective unconscious or universal pool of invisible thoughts and patterns. An example is when humanity falls asleep, we forget that we are spiritual beings. However, each mind that becomes conscious awakens the collective.

These principles help us understand synchronicity or coincidences. A friend comes to mind and the phone rings. Though we may be surprised to hear the friend on the other end, the connection has occurred because of interacting minds acting like radio transmitters. We may not visibly see radio waves when we tune a channel but we know they exist. We may not see our thoughts but we can observe them in action if we pay attention.

The Guiding Power of Spirit uses our powerful mind to receive instructions and roadmaps. The signals may initially be faint, but with fine-tuning and a still mind, we can increase the reception. Guidance is ever-present. An open mind allows us to hear the messages. Every time we tune into our GPS and follow the instructions, we allow the vehicle of our mind to be directed with purpose, direction and will.

Take another moment and check in with your mind.

Mental Inventory

- Are you comfortable with your thoughts?

- Do you entertain more positive, loving thoughts or critical, fearful ones?

- Are you open to change your beliefs?

- In what ways are you able to shift negative thoughts and beliefs to more uplifting ones?

- Can you think of ways in which your thoughts help you connect with Spirit?

Relational Home

Relationships represent assignments made by Divine Intelligence, bringing together those who represent the greatest opportunities for learning from each other. – Marianne Williamson

One of our primary needs is to belong and feel loved. Infants immediately establish an attachment to a mother or caregiver. That attachment creates a pattern and becomes a building block in future relationships. If we felt protected, secure and loved, we would bring those memories to relationships. If we developed anxious or avoidant attachments, we would become fearful with intimacy.

Though our caregivers may not have provided us with the most loving experiences, we can overcome past conditioning if we move inward toward our True Self where our natural state is love. From that place, we can extend love to others and receive love in return. This creates a genuine, heartfelt bond and deepens our sense of belonging. Our heart can open and we can experience oneness rather than separateness.

That connection to others is the meaning of the relational home. With relationships that come from our heart, not from our ego, we generate peace and well-being. We naturally move toward unconditional love and the highest good. The realization that we are innate beings of light causes cooperation.

We recognize that resonance and dissonance are part of any relationship and that setting appropriate boundaries are acts of love, for they acknowledge that we can't fulfill everyone's desires. When we remain mindful of the expansion of our heart and of healthy boundaries, we become more comfortable expressing our True Self in relation to other Selves.

When Abraham Maslow researched the qualities of self-actualized persons, he found that their relationships tended to be deeper and more profound. They were capable of greater love and their ego boundaries dissolved. He also found there was a deeper sense of compassion for the whole of mankind.

Humans exude great compassion for those who suffer even if they're in other countries. Despite cultural or political differences, people come together in the face of shared tragedy. Natural disasters often stimulate an outpouring of help from around the globe and remind us that we are all brothers and sisters. Many of us have had experiences of being touched deeply by strangers. When we connect from the heart, we can be at home with anyone.

Our GPS uses the vehicle of relationships to spread love into the community. Spirit guides us to the right people to help us on our journeys. Some may assist us in healing relational wounds; others will strengthen the feeling of love and belonging. Our only mission is to stay in our heart.

Take a few moments and check in with your heart.

Relational Inventory

- Are you comfortable relating with others?

- Can you give and receive love?

- What aspects of your relationships need attention or clarification of boundaries?

- What types of relationships satisfy you the most?

- Can you think of ways in which your relationships connect with Spirit?

Expressive Home

The voice of the intellect is a soft one but it does not rest till it has gained a hearing. – Sigmund Freud

The home of voice is the vehicle of communication and self-expression. It is the way we deliver our messages to the outside world. We communicate thoughts and feelings through words, song, prose, dialogue and non-verbal action. We may write in a journal, speak on a cell phone, relate a story, or gently touch a loved one. Whatever the medium, the intention is to express ourselves.

As social animals we are programmed to share our world. Communication is a vehicle to bond with others, exchange information, and satisfy needs and desires. However, since we were instructed as children how to use our voices, some of our voices may be shut down while others boom out of control.

Speaking our truth means authentically sharing our thoughts and feelings to others. Using our voice requires honesty and courage to openly reveal ourselves without judgment or condemnation. Uninhibited, without the need for others' approval, we become channels for Spirit.

Our GPS remains in constant communication with us and downloads information for us to express. We may be asked to share messages of forgiveness and love. A musician may be guided to play a song, a writer may be instructed to create a story, a healer may be asked to dispense advice, or a painter may be encouraged to splash colors on canvas. We all receive the call to share our lives and express our Inner Truth.

Take another moment to check in with your voice.

Expressive Inventory
• Are you comfortable expressing yourself?
• How do you communicate your needs, wants and desires?
• How can you be more honest with yourself and others?
• What forms of self-expression provide joy and satisfaction?
• How do you communicate with Spirit?

Visional Home

Vision is freely given to those who ask to see. – A Course in Miracles

The home of vision is about seeing from within – insight. It makes visible our inherent talents, gifts and dreams, and weaves them together with imagination and creativity for a Divine purpose. Our ultimate purpose is to serve Spirit and embrace love and inner peace. That requires an expanded vision.

To expand our vision, we must expand our consciousness. When we open our third eye, we recognize the invisible web where life is interconnected. Vision offers us the power of reflection to see what normally cannot be seen. It's about exploring the deeper realms of humanity and discovering who we are. It's about using intuition as a guiding light so we can penetrate illusions, tap an inner knowing, and enter the place of revelation and Holy Truths.

Vision is also about vocation, which comes from the Latin noun *vocatio*, meaning summons. The word suggests that we are summoned by the Divine to make a unique contribution on Earth. We may be called to create a business, teach children, or write prose. We can narrow our focus by adopting a mission, such as promoting an inspiring message or healing the planet. The mission leads us back to our broader vision.

Our GPS will show us what we need, where we're meant to go, what we're supposed to do and who we're supposed to meet. Once we surrender old images and perceptions, we can open our eyes and truly see.

Take another moment and check in with your vision.

Vision Inventory

- Are you comfortable with your personal mission and vision?

- Do you recognize your talents and life purpose?

- What elements of your mission or vision need redirection?

- How do you nurture imagination and intuition?

- Can you think of ways in which your talents, purpose and vision connect you with Spirit?

MAPPING EXERCISE

Before beginning the first mapping exercise, you may want to obtain a journal so you can record your responses. The journal will help you keep track of the many places you'll visit. Some exercises will require time to stop by the roadside for reflection; others will call for spontaneous responses.

The Home Inventory will help you increase your self-awareness so you can assess your current life and notice the patterns in your physical, emotional, mental, relational, expressive and visional homes. Honest review is necessary before you can make any decisions about altering your course. Therefore, complete this inventory with the attitude that the correct answer is what rings true. In each row select a statement that most reflects how you currently view yourself.

Home Inventory					
I tend to neglect my body.		I actively care for my body.		I tend to become preoccupied with my body.	
I'm not very aware of my senses and have difficulty experiencing pleasure.		I enjoy my senses and feel alive.		I need a lot of sensory stimulation to feel alive.	
I feel cut off from my feelings.	(	I am at ease with my feelings.	/	I tend to be highly sensitive.	
I tend to suppress my emotions.		I manage my emotions well.		I can swing from emotional highs to lows.	
I tend to be a pessimist.	/	I see both the obstacles and the opportunities.		I am almost always optimistic.	
I tend to be quite definite in my opinions.	/	I have an inquisitive and open mind.		My opinions can be easily swayed.	
When completing projects, I am highly disciplined.	/	It's easy to focus on projects and accomplish them.		I tend to procrastinate.	
I prefer being alone.	/	I feel connected with others and set clear boundaries.		I tend to overwhelm others and often have difficulty with boundaries.	
I tend to be very competitive.	)	I enjoy cooperative relationships.		I tend to sacrifice my own needs in relationships.	/
I tend to be shy and inhibited.		I openly share my life with others.		I really enjoy the spotlight.	
I keep my thoughts and opinions to myself.	/	I easily share my thoughts and opinions with others.		I make sure my opinions are heard.	
I have difficulty being direct with others.	/	When communicating, I enjoy listening and sharing.	\	I often get impatient listening to others.	
I have difficulty giving and receiving.		I freely give and receive.	↑	I often make sure that my needs are met.	
I lack direction in my life.		I have a clear vision, purpose and direction.	\	I have many dreams and aspirations but have difficulty taking action.	
I often don't recognize my talents and gifts and am dissatisfied with my life path.		I feel inspired and creative and incorporate my talents into a life purpose.	↑	I am continually marketing my life and my services.	
Total		Total	10	Total	2

When you've completed the inventory, total the number that you checked under each of the three columns. The column on the left indicates that you tend to adapt to the world by holding on, contracting, shutting down and erecting protective barriers. The column on the right indicates that you tend to adopt a more excessive state of letting loose, indulging, obsessing and becoming absorbed in the world. Higher scores in either the right or left columns highlight patterns you may wish to change. The middle column shows the golden mean with a balanced natural state of being at home. You might slide across the spectrum and discover some areas that are balanced and others that require counter-balancing. This inventory can then act as a rough guide to review your current course and present alternative routes.

We'll discuss these columns more fully in the following chapters. For now, log the entries in your journal. You can refer back to them later and highlight any changes.

GUIDED VISUALIZATION

Guided visualizations can expand your consciousness. They work best when you're in a relaxed space free of distractions such as cell phones. You can treat visualizations as reading meditations. You could read the visualization and then close your eyes to deepen the images. You could also record the visualization and play it back at your leisure. Alternately, you could ask a partner to read the visualization while you relax into his or her voice. Consider playing soothing music and lighting a candle to accentuate the mood.

The visualizations are organized to take you on different routes that, ultimately, will take you Home. Use your imagination to create your own personal inward journey. Allow the images to unfold and access your many senses. Let us begin:

Make yourself comfortable and take a deep breath. Hold it a moment, then exhale, letting go of all the tension. Take another deep breath. Hold it a moment. Then exhale, releasing any stress and worry. Take another deep breath. Hold it, then exhale, releasing doubts, fears and anxieties. Let them disappear and dissolve. With each breath, allow yourself to go deeper so you can become more conscious of your different homes. Allow whatever happens to happen. There is no right or wrong.

As you move into a gentle rhythm of breathing, become aware of your body. This is your physical home. Notice the areas where you feel tension or tightness. There may be places where you hold stress. With each exhalation, allow the tension to dissolve. Notice the places in your body where you feel comfortable. Allow your breath to expand your connection with all your senses. You have the right to experience sensual pleasure. You have the right to be supported as your body carries you through life.

Now allow your awareness to shift to your emotional home. You have the right to feel, so allow any emotions to surface into awareness. There is no right or wrong. There just is. Notice your emotions. Honor them. Allow them to become your teachers. You may feel comfortable with some feelings and uncomfortable with others. Your emotional home adds color and texture to your life.

When you're ready, shift your awareness to the home of your mind. It helps you think, process the world, and make decisions. Notice whether your mind is busy or quiet. Observe your thoughts. They show you what's going on in your mind. Watch your thoughts as if they are passing clouds. You have a beautiful mind. Know that you have the right to think and exercise your will.

When you're ready, shift to your relational home. Bring your attention to your heart. Notice if there are any constrictions around your heart that prevent you from giving or receiving love. Breathe love into your chest and allow your heart to expand. Just allow whatever happens to happen. You have the right to unconditional love. Inhale that love and let it circulate through your body and into all of your cells.

And when you're ready, shift your attention to your expressive home. Breathe into your throat, knowing that you have the right to express yourself and be heard. Notice if you have any inhibitions. Notice also a desire to communicate and share your experiences. With each breath, feel the connection with your voice and your inner truth. The world is waiting to hear from you.

When you're ready, bring your awareness to the home of inner vision. Imagine an eyelid opening to your third eye. This allows you to see through the fog of illusions and recognize your talents, creativity and Divine purpose. Allow any visions to emanate from your third eye. Insight flows into your life. You have the right to see your True Self and be acknowledged by others. You are perfect just the way you are.

Now imagine a loving Divine light flowing down through the top of your head. The loving light flows down through all of your homes: your visional, expressive, relational, mental, emotional and physical homes. Receive the loving connection as it circulates around your eyes, your voice, your heart, your mind, your feelings and your body. Realize that you are never alone but rather connected with an Infinite Source of Wisdom. Feel the light pouring into your many homes. Receive the love. Feel the peace. Enjoy the sacred space.

When you're ready to step back into the material world, prepare yourself for the return. You may feel limitation and constriction, but you now have a way to connect with your True Self. Home remains inside of you. It is everywhere and anywhere. You can always return to that place of unconditional love and inner peace.

Hold onto that peace and love and slowly bring yourself back into present time, ready to continue with the rest of the day, feeling refreshed and rejuvenated. As you become aware of your surroundings, stretch your arms and legs and allow yourself to become fully present.

When you are ready, take a few moments to record any significant thoughts, feelings or images in your journal.

CHAPTER TWO

ADAPTATION

The socialization process functions like a prison, a restraint more

powerful than our inner drive to wholeness.

– Harville Hendrix

Imagine you are a tiny baby attached to an umbilical cord, float-ing in warm, nurturing fluid. You receive everything you desire – nourishment, protection and unconditional love. Living inside your mother, you enjoy a regulated environment that monitors your temperature and bodily needs and satisfies them easily and lovingly. Then you are born. Thrust into the physical world, you lose your comfortable, safe haven. You now must rely on your in-nate physical senses. You must inform the world when you are cold or hot, hungry or uncomfortable. Thus begins the stage of adaptation.

Each birth replicates the story of the Garden of Eden and the loss of innocence. It begins the descent into the physical plane. After tasting the apple, Adam and Eve lost their paradise and com-promised their union with the Divine. They learned about separ-ateness, limitations, restrictions and disconnection. They became ashamed of being naked and took on clothes.

We were born naked and soon began to clothe ourselves with the beliefs of family, culture and society. Such limitations made it harder to see, hear or feel the Guiding Power of Spirit. They did, however, provide lessons. They taught us about the power of beliefs in a sensory, material world.

We arrived with the pre-installed genetic operating system for humans. Our in-built processors recorded our senses, emotions, thoughts, relationships, sounds and sights. We downloaded our caregivers' software programs and imported their virtues and viruses.

Over time, we created files, consisting of our parents' expectations and disappointments. We recorded when we felt loved or unloved, appreciated or punished. We adopted a language, culture, customs, nationality and values. Once we attended school, we downloaded more software about achievement, success and failure. We learned to accommodate and adapt in our material world. In the process we formed an identity composed of other people's beliefs. An eight-year-old boy in Iraq will develop a different world view from a child born in India or Brazil. And within a country, diverse regions and religious backgrounds will teach children to adopt a unique set of beliefs and behaviors.

Everyone creates their own version of the truth based on their learning and experience. Numerous facets shape one's belief system, including family circumstances, culture, birth order, gender, economic status, ethnic background, religion, genetic predisposition and society at large. Even the seasons are relative depending on our birth place. Those born in the Northern Hemisphere celebrate spring in March while those Down Under prepare for autumn. Life is truly a series of perceptions based on experiences and beliefs.

This is demonstrated in the story about a young girl who approached her mother while she was preparing breakfast. "Why do you cut bacon into tiny strips?" asked the daughter. The mother responded emphatically, "That's what my mother taught me." When the grandmother visited the family later in the week, the young girl asked her why bacon was cut into tiny strips. "I don't know," answered the grandmother. "That's what my mother taught me." As it so happened, the great grandmother was still alive. When the girl next visited her, she questioned her about the bacon. The aged woman scratched her puzzled face and thought for awhile. Then the light bulb went on. "Honey, we were so poor we could only afford a small frying pan."

Our caregivers downloaded into us their beliefs and attitudes, some of which initially served a purpose like the small frying pan. Through the process of adaptation we have unconsciously formatted countless files pertaining to the body, emotions, thoughts, relationships, communication and perceptions. However, programs that no longer serve us still run in the background.

To illustrate the adaptation process, I'll use a metaphor that came to me as I watched a window salesman demonstrate the benefits of his products. He placed an energy gauge two feet away from a heat lamp. Without any glass the gauge registered 300. The salesman then placed an inferior window 1/16th of an inch thick between the gauge and the heat lamp. The gauge dropped to 150. He replaced that window with one comprised of two 1/16th inch glass panes with argon gas. The gauge dropped to 50. He then replaced that window with his top-of-the-line product that consisted of two panes of 1/8th inch glass with argon gas. The gauge dropped to 5 and proved that thicker glass plus argon gas was far superior in blocking the sun's rays in summertime and retaining the heat in winter.

If each of our six homes – physical, emotional, mental, relational, expressive and visional – had windows through which Spirit shines light, then the level of illumination would depend upon the density and clarity of the glass. Unfortunately, the adaptation process tends to smudge our windows with countless fingerprints or beliefs. Suppressed pain and negative thoughts darken thick windows and block the light from illuminating our lives. We then become disconnected from Spirit.

With this concept in mind, let's explore adaptation and the windows of our six homes.

1. Physical Home. Our body chronicles the world of sensation. It teaches us about cause and effect. "Because I do this, something happens." We grew up learning about nutrition, self-care, sex, sensuality, pleasure and pain. If we were punished as children for not eating spinach, we would associate pain with the leafy green vegetable and gag at the very thought of consuming it. We filed away all of our experiences and, in the process, forged beliefs about our body. If we were raised with nurturance, our bodies would be wired for nurturing. If we experienced childhood trauma, our bodies would be wired for stress. As we adapted to our environment, we adopted ways to relieve the stress and tension. We found physical comfort in a variety of areas including food, sports, exercise, nature, touch, sex, sleep, alcohol or drugs.

Some forms of physical relief bring us back to our senses while others either satisfy cravings or shut down the senses. Those habits and beliefs that we adopted create a window for the light of Spirit. A grimy, neglected window blocks the light, while a clear glass illuminates our physical home.

2. Emotional Home. During the adaptation process, we discovered what feelings were and were not appropriate. When we were children and expressed emotions, such as sadness, anger, laughter, fear or joy, our parents responded in ways that either encouraged or discouraged feelings. A little girl might tell her father that she was mad at him but hear a dismissive comment, "Don't act that way." The child may come to believe that something was inherently wrong with her and may begin to numb herself whenever she felt angry. If the girl's mother rarely expressed anger, she might also expect the little girl to avoid conflict.

Since our caregivers were our models, we often mimicked their behaviors. At the same time, the cause-and-effect principle established patterns. If the girl once cracked a joke and noticed everyone laughing, she might use humor whenever she wanted attention. If no one laughed, she might resort to some other attention-getting device. Over time, our experiences and parental modeling taught us how to manage feelings. They created the filter for the window to our emotions. The stains of suppressed, painful feelings can block Spirit's healing beams, whereas acceptance, openness and transparency allow Spirit to shine.

3. Mental Home. Like a computer, our mind processes incredible amounts of information. We adapted by downloading files from numerous sources, storing them in memory banks, and retrieving them as needed.

When we were young, we were taught to accept those in authority and follow their instructions and beliefs as the truth. Once we began school, we obediently added more software and files.

We learned skills of language and mathematics as well as a view of history. The very structure and syllabus of the educational system shaped our thinking. An Islamic school would portray history from a different perspective than would a Catholic school in Ireland or a public school in China. And let's not forget the role that the media play with a curriculum based on negative news and fear-based stories. Religious beliefs can provide a counter-balance but even then, some faiths focus on damnation and retribution.

When I was a boy, I was taught by the Catholic Church that it was a mortal sin to eat meat on Friday. When the church revised the law and said it was no longer a sin worthy of condemning a soul to hell, I realized that doctrines were not based on fact and could be changed. After all, the church at one time prevented Galileo from publishing his scientific theories in the field of astronomy and only later recognized his truth.

We continue to store many outdated files in our minds. Limiting or negative thoughts and beliefs smudge our windows and obstruct Spirit from enlightening our mental home.

4. Relational Home. Relationships teach us about attachment, trust, acceptance, recognition and love. When we were children, we adopted behaviors to satisfy those needs. We may have discovered that pleasing people brought acknowledgement or rebelling brought attention, that withdrawal brought safety or relating brought love and affection. Through our interactions with our parents and other members in the family, we forged a template based on our family's relational model. We made decisions about letting others into our heart and defending against intruders, about cooperating and competing, about conflict and intimacy, about boundaries and lack thereof. We downloaded those circumstances when we received love and when we were punished and stored them in our memory banks.

Our powerful relational program, which is often unconscious, drives us to select partners and recreate patterns. Unfortunately, many of those internalized files do not lead to heartfelt love. Rather, they often create a mud-spattered window that prevents our hearts from receiving loving rays of sunshine.

5. Expressive Home. To access relationships we must communicate. As soon as we were born, our cries announced to the world that we had a voice and that we would express our needs. As we began to use that voice, we learned about language, grammar and etiquette. We chose certain words and phrases and discarded others. Some of us received praise every time we talked; others received scorn whenever we raised our voice. Our upbringing shaped the way we shared information and expressed our needs. Since we were rewarded and punished for certain language, statements or requests, we quickly detected when it was safe to be honest. We conformed and adapted and adjusted our speech, often hiding our truth. A voice coach, Jonathan Morgan Jenkins, highlighted this in his observation, "How often we take our voice for granted and fail to nurture it, or worse, abuse it."

When we dialogue with another, we open a two-way channel of communication. This involves negotiation: which subjects are discussed; who speaks and who listens; how decisions are made; who has power. Our training begins in the laboratory of the family. Similar to learning a language, we rely on repetition as a training tool and develop communication styles that affect the way we present ourselves, articulate our messages, respond to others, and satisfy our needs. These patterns remain with us until we consciously scrub the window and embrace the light.

6. Visional Home. Once we develop language, our perception and vision expand. However, well before we were born, our parents projected onto us their hopes and fears. They had expectations about roles, gender, career, relationships, money, spirituality, and so on. If we merged our talents and aspirations with their plans and satisfied their dreams, we were probably rewarded. If our ideas conflicted with theirs, we may have found ourselves in a struggle to either accommodate their wishes or nurture our own vision.

If we chose a career for the sake of our parents or to spite our parents, we may have pursued an unfulfilling path. If, on the other hand, we were encouraged to realize our true potential, we would have expanded our ability to see within and know our purpose. Unfortunately, when our ideas or dreams are deemed as unimportant, we become invisible. It's hard to envision a connection with Spirit when the window is painted black.

When we view all six windows, we recognize the true impact of adaptation. The accumulated beliefs regarding the body, emotions, thoughts, relationships, expression and perception have defined who we are. As children we readily downloaded files and programs, both valuing and devaluing, which, in turn, shaped our identity. In essence, we were hypnotized into believing that our ego, or "false self," was real. Our growing library of mental film-clips kept replaying on our internal screen, embedding the messages further. Of course, that reinforced an ego that constructed psychological defenses as protection. Adapting to a material world, the prodigal son packed his bag and left home.

In my childhood I collected plenty of beliefs about struggle and insecurity. My grandparents migrated from Poland and experienced the Depression. For them, growing up was about suffering and hardship. My parents adopted a similar mode of survival. They coped by working exceptionally hard. All else was secondary. When my father became mentally ill, the intense conflict between my parents created chaos and trauma. I adapted by becoming hyper-vigilant about their moods. This prepared me for flight in case of violence. I craved love and attention but was wary about my caregivers who could easily step into blame and attack. To survive, I shut down at an early age and became independent and self-reliant. I got myself off to school, organized my homework, and created an internal cave where I could retreat in the face of conflict.

Like my parents, I accepted that life was a struggle. My mother's hands were always full. There was never enough time in the day to accomplish all the tasks. Therefore, she would often tell her children, "Don't just sit there, do something." As a result, she rarely gave herself permission to relax. I remember entering the house one afternoon and finding her sitting on the couch and watching television. As soon as my mother saw me, she jumped up and returned with a vengeance to the ironing board and the mountain of clothes.

Following my mother's dictum, I learned to do lots of somethings. I neglected many emotional needs and chose busyness as a way to avoid trouble, and that included feeling my pain. I adopted a stoic work ethic and became more comfortable "doing" than "being." I became entranced in the self-fulfilling prophesy "Life *is* a struggle."

Interestingly, that same pattern has continued with my mother who is 96 years old. Regrettably, she has dementia. However, whenever I ask her how she's doing, she usually replies, "I'm very busy organizing things." When a belief becomes so entrenched in a mind, it gets repeated even when the mind fails.

To this day I have a tendency toward workaholism. I can easily get caught in a flurry of activity. I am more conscious now when I enter the trance state of busyness but to reverse the pattern, I offer myself an alternative with a periodic reminder, "Don't just sit there, do nothing!"

There is always the temptation to blame our caregivers. Remember, they gave us their very best. They were also hypnotized by programs and viruses passed down from previous generations. They believed in the downloaded pictures on their projection screens and couldn't recognize the viral images running in the background.

Yet even with the outmoded programs and files, our caregivers, more often than not, offered positive experiences and lessons that shaped our world. My mother made countless sacrifices to create a stable environment and feed and clothe her family. My grandmother offered a safe haven during the family firestorms. Though she didn't speak English well and couldn't offer words of love, my grandmother's helping hands and loving embrace taught me that somebody cared. Her Sunday pastries, school day lunches, and gentle manner offered a counter-balance to the anxious work-driven environment of my home.

The positive and negative patterns of the past are continually replicated until we choose otherwise. We can delete programs and even upload new software to replace corrupted files; however, while we're entranced in the adaptive mode, we rarely consider that as an option.

In order to shift out of adaptation, we must become aware of our programming. Since the outer world is a projective screen for our thoughts, we can view our internal software and files by observing what we see, hear and feel. Consciousness is the interface between the internal and external worlds.

Picture Times Square in New York City. Four people walk on a sidewalk at approximately the same time. The first person is a business woman in financial trouble. As she walks, she notices banks and financial institutions and wonders how she'll keep her business afloat. The second individual is an actor late for a casting call. He walks briskly and catches sight of every clock as he worries about missing his golden opportunity. The third person is a fashion designer who casually strolls past the fashion stores and assesses each garment on display. The fourth individual is a sailor on shore leave. His eyes wander to all the pretty girls.

While the four people appear in the same scene, each perceives whatever is on their mind. Their internal state dictates where they go, what they see and hear, whom they attract, and how they feel. Everything is relative to the way they perceive the world. And the way they perceive the world is dependent on the files and programs stored in their mental computers.

The law of attraction states that like attracts like. Beliefs and emotional states attract similar thoughts, people and experiences. Success breeds success. Misery loves company. Pregnant women start seeing other pregnant women around them. A man thinking of purchasing a BMW will notice a similar model appearing on the streets. We are drawn to similar friends and experiences.

At the same time, we are regulated by the principle of entrainment, namely, the tendency of organisms to establish rhythms together. If we live in a high-octane world of activity and senses, we will adopt that rhythm as the norm. For example, when we drive on a highway, we eventually travel with the flow of traffic. If most cars speed, we tend to follow suit. Women living in dormitories often menstruate around the same time. Tiny chicks placed together begin to chirp at the same frequency. Those attending a meditation weekend establish a relaxing group rhythm.

With these potent forces operating around us, it's easy to lose sight of our True Self. When our "false self" leads the way, we wander aimlessly. Like the prodigal son, we turn our attention outward for success and happiness. We erect darker and thicker panes of glass and feel the pain of separation. Having lost our way, we move further away from Home and enter the next stage of the journey, **Becoming an Orphan**.

MAPPING EXERCISE

There are two mapping exercises presented here will help you explore your embedded beliefs and behaviors. The second exercise will take longer, as it asks you to write a personal story.

Part One. The goal of this exercise is to reveal some of the layers of beliefs that you wear like clothes. They create your identity. In your journal, write the question, "Who am I?" Then without judgment, write as many responses as you can that begin with the phrase, "I am . . ." You may start off with roles like mother, lawyer, wife, grandfather, etc. Next, make a list of the positive traits that best describe you, such as, "I am compassionate, loving, generous, sensitive and successful." Imagine how others might describe your strengths and expand your list further. Once you record your positive traits, answer the question, "Who am I?" with any negative characteristics, such as, "I am fearful, stupid, unworthy and angry." Imagine how others would describe your weaknesses, and again expand the list.

Once you've recorded your roles and positive and negative traits, repeat the question, "Who am I?" Explore the additional the layers that compose your identity. Notice the many masks you wear.

Now move further inward, to a place of inner knowing. See if you can catch a glimpse of your True Self. Record any thoughts with the "I am . . ." phrase, such as, "I am love."

Part Two. Now that you've revealed some of the layers of your identity, you're ready to clarify your personal story. Consider your life as an amazing adventure. Write a one-page biography that encompasses your journey. Your narrative, or the way you describe your journey, shapes the way you view the past, live the present and perceive the future. Therefore, consider yourself as the hero or heroine on a quest. If you can, define your quest. Highlight the lessons you've learned and those you still need to learn. You can name the enemies or obstacles that taught you about adversity. You can list the allies and triumphs that heralded success.

As you write your biography, don't worry about getting it right. Remember, your story is an unfolding journey. Once you clarify your story, you can then shift your perspective and create a new narrative. We will discuss that later in a forthcoming chapter. For now, spend time on the current version of your story. See it as an adventure that will ultimately lead you back Home.

GUIDED VISUALIZATION

In a relaxing place, free of distractions, make yourself comfortable. You may want to light a candle and play relaxing music to set the mood. Bring your awareness to your breathing. Notice the gentle rhythm. Let your breathing guide your body to relax, taking you deeper within.

Imagine a golden light above the top of your head. A stream of loving energy pours over your head, relaxing, soothing and healing. Allow this golden light to gently travel down your body and progressively relax all the muscles, from the face down to your jaw, down your neck to the shoulders, down your arms, past your elbows to the tips of your fingers. The golden light gently moves down the trunk of your body, down your chest and your spine to your pelvis, down your hips, past your thighs. It travels down your legs all the way to your knees, then moves to your calves and ankles, and down to the soles of your feet.

Now move into your mind's eye and imagine yourself as a baby floating in warm, nurturing water. An umbilical cord connects you with your mother. You are protected, safe and loved. You float without judgment and without worry. You are a child of the universe, supported with unlimited potential. Loving energy flows to every cell of your body. You experience waves of peace.

When you're ready, allow yourself to prepare for birth. Contractions begin. You feel the pulse of life guiding you outside. You're ready to enter the world. Notice whether the delivery is easy or complicated. A premature birth or a cesarean section provides unique lessons. Notice how you move into the world and how you immediately begin to adapt and survive. Notice how you express your needs and how the world responds.

Your senses begin recording all your experiences. They are stored in an enormous library. There is a constant stream of sensory input that includes temperature, sound, light and pictures, touch, taste and smell. Notice these sensations.

Now consider your parents. They offer you a nationality, culture, language and family background. They have preconceptions about your gender and birth order. They have hopes and dreams for you even though you're only a baby. Observe what they want you to think and believe and how they want you to act. Note how you record everything and file the information in your library.

Now imagine yourself as a young child. Notice how you feel about being a boy or a girl, whether you follow in your parents' footsteps, and how you respond to their beliefs and behaviors. Notice also whether your caregivers encourage you to be yourself. When you act against their wishes, observe what happens. If love is threatened, notice how you react, and how you accommodate.

Observe how your library expands. You record the opinions and actions of your siblings, teachers and ministers. They add layers to your identity. There are countless video clips that shape the way you treat your body, feel emotion, think and exercise your will, relate to others, voice your ideas and perceive your world. Recognize the beliefs that cause you to shutter the windows to your soul. Also recognize that you can open the windows and embrace the Light.

As you raise the light of consciousness, you become more aware of the images and thoughts that you project outward. You welcome the light into your body, emotions, mind, heart, voice and vision. You bring that light with you as you slowly move back into present time.

When you are ready, take some deep breaths and allow yourself to become aware of your surroundings.

Take a moment to record your experience. Write about the familial, cultural and societal expectations that you stored in your library. How did they affect you physically, emotionally and mentally? How did they impact your relationships, your style of communication and your view of the world? At what age was your identity clearly defined? When did you lose sight of your True Self?

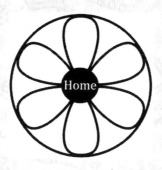

CHAPTER THREE

BECOMING AN ORPHAN

You, as the observer of a trauma, take a picture of it, hold it, merge with it,

go to sleep, and then go on the same tape-loop ride over and over again.

– Stephen Wolinsky

When I was born, the umbilical cord was wrapped around my neck, strangling me. My mother told me she wasn't sure I would make it because, upon delivery, I had turned blue. Thus began my entry into the world. Instead of a welcome embrace, I plopped into life struggling to breathe and survive.

Later in adulthood, I asked my mother about her early recollections of my birth. She confided that during her pregnancy with me my father left her for two weeks. With two young children already on her hands, she couldn't bear the thought of another child. Desperate, she believed she'd have a better chance looking after two children rather than three.

I could only imagine a distressed mother of two, pregnant with a third, abandoned by her husband. She must have been overwhelmed with anxiety and fear about her future, wondering if she'd survive. Money was scarce and a third child to feed and clothe would take up valuable resources. My mother confessed to me that during that difficult period, she prayed I wouldn't be born.

I'm grateful that prayer was never answered. Yet, I realize that emotionalized thoughts, such as prayers, create a major impact. I believe the umbilical cord curled around my neck was my mother's attempt to prevent me from entering a world fraught with uncertainty and fear.

We may reason that since a fetus doesn't think, it is oblivious to its surroundings. However, the fetus, with the DNA messages of both parents encoded in the genes, floats in the uterus, symbiotically entwined with the mother. The child receives nourishment passed through the umbilical cord. The fetus absorbs healthy nutrients as well as harmful drugs, depending on what is being transmitted. In addition, the child receives sensory input about a range of experiences including trauma. Though he or she doesn't process them on a cognitive level, the child knows them on a sensory level. That includes both love and emotional stress. If a mother feels love, so does the infant. If the mother feels grief, so does her child.

Dr. William Emerson, a pioneer in the field of prenatal and perinatal psychology, believed that trauma to the fetus can be laid down as early as conception and implantation.[1] The memory of the birth and earlier trauma is pre-cognitive and is imprinted in the body. This memory can establish patterns that continue into adulthood. They operate on an unconscious level yet dramatically impact lives.

If during birth, the disruption from a safe womb is severe and traumatic, it can result in a split. The psychologist Dr. John Rowan, who wrote extensively about birth trauma, discussed the split. "In a primitive and almost instinctual way, we dissociate into a hurt and vulnerable self that is hidden away and a less sensitive self that is pushed forward. . . . Once this split has occurred, its effects usually continue for a lifetime, as it pushes the individual to re-create repeatedly, in a myriad of ways, the original trauma, in failed attempts to master it."[2]

Thus begins the orphan's journey. When we sever the umbilical cord from our internal navigational system, we experience a split and become disconnected from Home. Dr. Emerson rightly pointed out that each of us has a core self that even severe trauma can't touch. And when trauma is resolved, we are left with our

True Self. We may not know that we lost that Home but, deep down, we feel a deep yearning for connection. As an orphan we set sail in a ship, lost in a fog and in the on-board chaos, unaware of the surrounding ocean of love.

In my case, the message of not belonging or being wanted was encoded as a powerful belief. My mother said that I was a very good baby because she could leave me alone and I would play by myself. That made her job as a stressed-out mother much easier. Clearly, I had learned not to place demands on a mother whose arms were full. I stifled my inner voice and fit in with a family coping with tremendous adversity. Since my existence was dependent on the family's survival, I endeavored to place few demands on my mother. My unconscious, however, craved attention and love and found somatic ways, such as severe eczema, to reveal itself. I didn't know it then but I was orphaned from the basic right to live a full life, which included acknowledging and expressing needs and desires. Fortunately, I also incorporated beliefs about overcoming adversity and surviving, just like my mother. Resilience became a saving attribute whenever I encountered difficulties.

By the time I was nine years old and visited Mooseheart with my mother and siblings, I knew that the child-care facility housed fellow orphans who were victims of a fate that neglected to bestow good fortune. I didn't realize then that all of us, in one way or another, become orphans.

An orphan is someone who moves furthest away from Home. In effect, the orphan shutters the windows to the Divine. Sitting in darkness, the orphan lives in the past and adopts the role of powerless victim. S/he identifies with the downloaded images playing in a relentless loop on the screen of the mind. The orphan often moves out of physical alignment and lapses into emotional upheaval, mental confusion, anxious relating, frantic talking, and blurred vision. S/he unknowingly perceives the self as separate from others.

When we become orphans, we relate from ego, the "false self," and repeat the same stories. We use denial and projection to defend against the fear, guilt, shame and despair that arise from the repetition of painful memories, chaining us to a feeling of separateness. Though the Guiding Power of Spirit emanates a beacon of light, we remain lost in the valley of shadows. Without access to the navigational system, we drive aimlessly and despairingly in a fog of illusions. As orphans, we become disillusioned and often resign ourselves to living helpless lives of desperation.

Unable to feel the connection with Home, we wander blindly, oblivious to the inner world, our life patterns, the myriad of available choices, and the beckoning heart of a loving Spirit. The downloaded files and viral programs separate us from our internal navigational system.

Seeking connection, the orphan longs for that perfect relationship to satisfy unmet needs and desires. Of course, frustration is inevitable, for no human can truly satisfy the longing for Home. Seeking to get plugged in, an orphan may switch on television or the Internet. These distractions often move him or her further into a trance state, sleepwalking through life. The average American watches about 160 minutes of television each day. That's over 900 hours per year, or 63,000 hours over 70 years, bombarding our psyche with images of separateness and fear.

After awhile, we forget we're orphans. This is represented in the riddle, "How do you know what you do not know when you do not know?" The only way to know what we don't know is to first know *that* we don't know. Then we can discover what we need to know. Since we've forgotten about Home, we must first recognize that we are lost.

During this stage, we experience separateness and longing. The longing makes us aware of the orphan state, when we moved out of range from our home base. Orphans take up residence in either a recessive state that involves holding on, contraction, isolation and restriction, or an excessive state of letting loose, over-indulgence, obsession and enmeshment. Of course, each extreme has some benefits. At one end, we learn to have and to hold, while the other end teaches us to let go and release. It's when we adhere to a rigid pattern that we move out of alignment.

The Home Base Chart highlights the polarities for the six petals of our flowering life.

HOME BASE CHART

Physical

Not at home Recessive	At home Balanced	Not at home Excessive
• Neglected body	• Delighted with body	• Obsessed with body
• Senses shut down	• Awakened senses	• Sensory addiction
• Rigid body, armored	• Grounded and expansive	• Ungrounded, flighty
• Detached from nature	• Connected to nature	• Overwhelmed by environment

Emotional

Not at home Recessive	At home Balanced	Not at home Excessive
• Cut off from feelings	• Awareness, acceptance and management of feelings	• Hypersensitive
• Suppressed emotions		• Excessive emotionality
• Joyless	• Ease with emotions	• Extreme highs or lows
	• Nurtures gratitude and joy	

Mental

Not at home Recessive	At home Balanced	Not at home Excessive
• Closed mind	• Inquisitive mind	• Drifting mind
• Cynical	• Processes information	• Gullible
• Dogmatic, rigid	• Focused and directed	• Procrastinates
• Forces will	• Willpower	• Ever-changing will

Relational

Not at home Recessive	At home Balanced	Not at home Excessive
• Closed heart	• Heart-centered connection	• Co-dependent
• Loneliness	• Love and Intimacy	• Few boundaries, enmeshed
• Isolated	• Sense of belonging	• Excessive need to belong
• Highly competitive	• Cooperative	• Sacrifices own need for others

Expressive

Not at home Recessive	At home Balanced	Not at home Excessive
• Inhibited	• Uninhibited innocence	• Exhibitionist
• Suppresses voice	• Expresses Inner Truth	• Obsessive need to be heard
• Indirect communication	• Honest communication	• Difficulty listening
• Difficulty giving and receiving	• Freely gives and receives	• Aggressively takes

Visional

Not at home Recessive	At home Balanced	Not at home Excessive
• Lack of direction	• Inner-directed Guidance	• Ego tries to direct Spirit
• Lack of vision	• Clarity of vision and purpose	• Illusions
• Uncreative, talents hidden	• Inspiration, insight and creativity	• Grandiosity
• Vocational uncertainty	• Vocation serves True Self	• Imposes own vision on others

As the chart demonstrates, home is the center and indicates a state of balance. The left side of home identifies the recessive state, while the right side highlights the excessive. We may be recessive in some areas or excessive in others. We could be shut down physically but express ourselves excessively in an exhibitionistic way.

We uniquely adapt to our own environments and constrict and expand in order to survive. A way of responding may serve us one time but not at others. Since the optimal state is balance, we may periodically swing like a pendulum to the opposite side before finding home base.

Let's explore each petal of our flowering life.

When we're at home *physically*, we delight in our body. Our awakened senses help us interact with the external world. We are grounded, expansive and connected to mother Earth. While orphaned, we can recede into a rigid, armored body that shuts down sensations, neglects physical signs and symptoms, and detaches from nature. At the other extreme, we can move into excess and become obsessed with the body, addicted to senses, ungrounded and flighty, and overwhelmed by the environment.

Our natural *emotional* home is a place where we're at ease with evolving emotions that provide feedback about our internal world. There is an awareness, acceptance and management of feelings as we nurture gratitude and joy. We become imbalanced when we suppress our emotions and live joylessly. At the other end of the spectrum, we can become hypersensitive and excessively emote in highs and lows.

When we are *mentally* at home, our inquisitive mind processes information and directs our attention with powerful focus. As orphans we can recede into a dogmatic, cynical, rigid and closed mind that tries to force will. Alternatively, we can naively consume ideas and concepts without discernment, and procrastinate with a confused, drifting mind and weak will.

The *relational* home has a heart-centered connection that embraces love and intimacy, a sense of belonging and a climate of cooperation. At the recessive extreme, a closed heart perpetuates competition, power struggles, loneliness and isolation. The opposite pole of excess is characterized by an overwhelming need to belong that creates co-dependent, enmeshed, self-sacrificing relationships with few boundaries.

The *expressive* home is a place of uninhibited innocence where we honestly communicate with others, express our inner truth, and freely give and receive. As orphans we can suppress our voices and inhibit self-expression, communicate indirectly, and have difficulty giving and receiving. At the opposite extreme, we can have an obsessive need to be heard, have difficulty listening, become exhibitionistic, and aggressively take from others.

Our natural *visional* home is about inner-directed guidance that helps us clarify our life vision, purpose and direction. From that place we access inspiration, insight, imagination and creativity. We recognize our gifts and wisely serve our True Self through a vocation that incorporates talents with purpose. When we operate out of the recessive state, we lack direction and vision, lose sight of our talents and creativity, and live a purposeless life. At the excessive extreme, our ego resides in grandiosity and illusions and tries to direct Spirit and impose its views on others.

Misalignments in the six realms result from our downloaded beliefs, experiences and responses and get replayed until we become conscious of the patterns. Embedded wounds from trauma can be the most difficult to recognize and shift.

In my own life, I survived a dysfunctional family by shutting down. I escaped into a mind of imagination and sought spiritual comfort from the Catholic faith. My seminary days during high school and college brought spiritual direction; however, I often felt disconnected from my body, emotions, heart and voice. By the time I was a senior in high school, I was overweight and felt emotionally alone and invisible – clearly an orphan. Without a forum to express my thoughts and feelings, I felt separate from others. I learned to self-soothe through food and fantasy. My refuge was spirituality. Visits to the chapel consoled me and brought moments of inner peace. But that would fade when the downloaded viral images resurrected childhood wounds.

Deep wounds like abandonment, neglect, shame or abuse splinter off parts of the psyche. The deepest wounds are inflicted when we're children. An arrow thrust into a large oak tree will produce a small hole, but shoot that same arrow at a green sapling and it will split it in half. Arrows embedded into innocent young hearts cause massive holes. Some wounds eventually heal; others leave permanent scars.

Since many of the wounds begin during a pre-cognitive state, they often get locked in the body. There is a causal relationship between early trauma and emotional and behavioral problems. A study published in Sweden in 1987, conducted by the Karolinska Institute, showed a correlation between early birth traumas, such as forceps delivery or oxygen deprivation, and the method of suicide. Statistics were gathered in Stockholm from the birth records of 412 forensic victims who died either from suicide or the effects of drug addiction or alcoholism between 1978 and 1984. The study compared this group to a control group of 2901 people and showed that "suicides involving asphyxiation were closely associated with asphyxia at birth; suicides by violent mechanical means were associated with mechanical birth trauma; and drug addiction was associated with opiate and/or barbiturate administration to mothers during labor."[3]

The early trauma can act like a rampant virus operating in the background. To survive the sensory imprint of trauma and childhood wounds, we cauterize the wounds and stem the blood flow by developing defense mechanisms and behavioral patterns. When the body is faced with extreme loss, inducing shock is a method of self-preservation. Blood flow and energy is diverted to the critical areas of the body. With traumatic emotional experiences, survival often means shutting down. While shock may offer a temporary means of survival, it is not the way we're meant to live. Unfortunately, orphans fall into psychological shock as a way of life.

When we deny wounds that are painful and gut-wrenching, they become the source of our destruction. A poisoned barb left embedded in the heart continues to emit toxins. Building calluses around the heart can stop it from bleeding, but the trapped, throbbing pain will silently develop into a raging infection. A more devastating secondary wounding occurs as a result of the silence, suppression, denial, projection and detachment from others.

Fears of suffering further wounds engender life-long patterns of orphaned behaviors – receding into shutting down or excessively satisfying cravings. Over time, this merely re-wounds the psyche and intensifies the orphaned state. When we deny the existence of deep, profound experiences, we disassociate our self from our body, emotions, mind, heart, voice and vision. An orphan erects towering walls that keep others away from the hurt and vulnerable self.

If we experience further losses during one or several of the developmental stages of life, we become psychologically stuck on the journey. We may abandon the quest toward Home and seek shelter in addictive, destructive or compulsive behaviors and dysfunctional relationships. Facing our orphaned parts offers the key to healing and freedom. Since embedded arrowheads in the heart can sever the aorta, finding the source of the wounds is a matter of life and death – for the human spirit.

One of my frightening childhood memories involved a violent argument between my parents. My father was threatening my screaming mother with a knife. My older brother and sister screamed and begged him to stop. I was just a little boy and stood frozen in terror, watching this horror movie. The knife was eventually relinquished without spilled blood, but the sheer trauma of the episode made me feel powerless, unprotected and unsafe. My father was supposed to be my protector, yet he acted as the destroyer. I decided then that survival meant shutting down the unbearable pain of witnessing parents on the path of destruction. I buried my thoughts and feelings, hoping they would become invisible, and developed a pattern of busyness that replicated my family's coping mechanism.

As a therapist, I have heard dreadful stories from many a client who faced the dark night of the soul and yearned for protection. Such personal stories take on greater magnitude when they involve a society. Displaced cultures, like the American Indians forced onto reservations, the Jews sent to concentration camps, or the stolen generation of half-caste Aborigines relocated to mission schools, can produce generations of orphans seeking a place to call their own.

If you felt like an orphan, it would be natural to feel anxious, insecure, frightened and unloved. You may have survived by disconnecting from one or even several of the six petals of your flowering life. Your mind might have erected a museum of horrors that represented your lost childhood. You may have shuttered the doors to the past hoping to forget those dark nights of the soul. However, any reminder of previous wounds could act as a trigger and toss you back into the house of shadows.

When I went through my divorce, I flashed back to the horrific battles of my parents and the resulting devastation of the family. I actually visualized a museum in the basement of a house. Charred beams were scattered on the ground of a basement that had no windows or light. A burnt trap door on the floor led to a tiny crawl space which offered safety for my orphan, a little boy terrified by the fires of raging parents. The orphan's face and rag-torn clothes were smudged with soot. He survived in that tiny hole. Though the fire no longer raged outside, fear remained inside. The only escape was to leave the familiar charred remains of fear and climb the winding staircase to freedom and peace.

That was the image of my orphan whom I call little Lenny. Attacks or conflict threw him back into a hum of anxiety. The sight of any large knife could trigger memories that increased the internal hum. That humming would suck him into the dark, dingy basement. To manage the anxiety, he retreated into a world of imagination and became a consummate reader of comics that portrayed superheroes protecting the world from horrible villains.

It may be obvious to imagine an orphan who was abandoned or rejected, but consider also the opposite extreme, those who experienced overprotection, overindulgence and an overwhelming sense of entitlement. We tend not to think of such children as orphans, but remember that those who are self-absorbed with an inflated ego also lose their authentic Self.

Consider Siddhartha who was born in a palace, protected by his parents from witnessing poverty, illness, suffering or death. He felt compelled to leave his material wealth and wandered for years until he found the Home of enlightenment as the Buddha under the Bodhi tree.

Like Siddhartha, we will wander as orphans until we become aware that we are unconscious, in a trance. Then we can know what we need to know. We can recognize that the shutters on our windows have been closed and awaken our deep longing to move out of darkness and return Home.

Homelessness then becomes a motivating force. It's also a source of incredible gifts. In darkness, quests are born, books are written, missions are created, lives are reborn. Like a tiny seed buried underground, the orphan pushes upward toward the light of awareness and brings incredible gifts.

In my own life, little Lenny beckoned me to find my voice and recognize my talents. Not surprisingly, I entered the healing profession. There's an old saying that those who become therapists do so because we need 40 hours of therapy a week. We attract clients who help us with our own healing. We also reflect back what we most need to hear. As a result of working with clients and their inner orphans, I have healed many aspects of myself. When I listened to my own advice, I heard myself encourage others to connect with their bodies, accept their emotions, shift their beliefs, love themselves and others, express their pain and gratitude, expand their vision, and listen to their inner guidance.

Little Lenny also needed healing through self-expression. He guided me to journal, write books, and share my story. And when a poem needed to be birthed, words captured a mood. During a bleak period of my life, I wrote the poem *Skeleton Man*, a bare bones description of the orphan stage.

> *Alone,*
> *I traveled the road often traveled*
> *Doing what should be done,*
> *Expecting what others expect,*
> *Adapting to what others want.*
>
> *Seeking safety and comfort,*
> *I retreat into the body's prison,*
> *As my spirit moves into slumber,*
> *The dark night of the soul.*
>
> *Within the caverns of my psyche*
> *Lies a deep, ravenous hunger.*
> *A hunger that gnaws at my spirit,*
> *Shredding my entrails, eviscerating my flesh.*

My emptiness cries aloud,
"Where are you, oh God?"
"Where is your compassion?"
"Your love and protection?"

God offers a reply. Silence.

I walk the burnt and blistered desert,
Seeking a home.
Plodding, sometimes crawling,
My decimated body hangs limp, exhausted.
Flesh tormented, again and again.
I walk no more and surrender, a skeleton man.

Now clanking and clinking to the whims of the wind,
My skeleton lies in wait.
Bones bleached by the scorching sun,
My skull, home to the scorpions of the night.
I wait – listening, praying – I wait
For a whisper of hope.

Days bleed into nights.
Hope gives way to despair.
My clinking, clanking bones chime with the wind,
Sounding a toll.
A toll warning travelers,
Beware of forgotten souls.

Time turns into eternity.
A windswept mound entombs my bones,
Harboring deathly silence.
An empty socket peeps through the sand,
It remains open to the sky
And the scorpions of the night.

When the moon spins black, a she-snake stirs.
Gliding on ebony skin, she scours the desert for a home.
Cautious, yet ferocious, she slithers into a skull,

Only to be met by a scorpion – her first meal.
She burrows deeper where sand gives way to a spine.
A mate has been found!

Hungry for love, she encircles the vertebrae,
Caressing the spine, writhing in ecstasy.
Yet, she receives no response, not even a tremor.
Never before has she been so ignored.
She shovels through sand, fangs at the ready
And attacks the lifeless serpent.

A two-pronged bite punctures the coccyx.
Venom of black ink mixes with marrow
Causing the bones to shudder
And skeleton man to stir.

Pain, a deep resounding pain,
Thumps up each vertebra
Till a rhythm of drum beats pound in my skull.
The pain of unmet needs, wants, and desires
Transmutes an awakening.
Visions of joy pierce my soul.

The marrow transfuses life.
Organs appear, arteries pump red blood,
Flesh begets sumptuous flesh.
I rise from the desert tomb.

With my spirit transformed
I breathe my first breath.
I step into the light of day.
Power surges through my bones.
The sand falls from my eyes; I can see.
My God, you have not forsaken me.

Poetry and prose offered a format to express myself in symbolism and metaphor. In addition to my writing, I have received other special gifts from the orphan. One of the most significant was a burning desire to give my children a better experience of fatherhood. The innocent eyes and beautiful spirits of my daughter, Melissa, and my son, Nate, showed me what I had missed in my childhood. That propelled me forward in my own healing.

The diamonds are within us, ready to be mined. Therefore, it's imperative that we enter the darkness and discover our little orphans. They will tell us when we ignore our body, feelings, thoughts, relationships, voice and vision, and show us what we need to get back into alignment. They will remind us about early deficits so we can heal those lost parts of ourselves and access our core, our True Self, where trauma never penetrates.

Unfortunately, the distress signals from our orphans may be difficult to see, hear or feel when we're shut down, overwhelmed, disconnected, inhibited, invisible and alone. We may be sleeping at three in the morning but, rest assured, it's only a matter of time before the sun peeps over the horizon and the alarm clock rings to signal the next stage of awakening – **Wake-up Calls and Signposts.**

MAPPING EXERCISE

The following list of questions will bring your childhood experience into awareness. Review the list and respond to the ones that seem most pertinent, answering in the *present tense*, as if you are a young child. Using the present tense moves you back in time so that you can evoke those childhood thoughts and feelings. Choose an age that calls to you. It may be a time before kindergarten or after you started school. It could be your adolescence. You could review old photos, movies or video clips to stimulate your memory. Your responses will help you identify your orphaned parts. Record whatever comes to mind.

If the present tense creates too much emotional discomfort, you can create emotional distance by answering the questions in the past tense so that your adult self reflects back on your past.

AS A YOUNG CHILD:

1. Are you happy you are a girl/boy? Do you have a nickname?
2. How do you feel about your body?
3. Name the parts of your body that you feel most proud? Most ashamed?
4. What sensory experiences stand out in you mind?
5. Do you feel connected to nature and your home environment?
6. What feelings are appropriate and not appropriate?
7. What is the happiest moment you remember about your childhood?
8. What is the saddest moment?
9. Who punishes you? Do you deserve it? Why/Why not?
10. What makes you feel neglected, abused, lost or forgotten?
11. Who rewards you? For what do you receive rewards?
12. What is the best reward anyone can give you?
13. Are you encouraged to think for yourself?
14. Do you have more fearful or uplifting thoughts?
15. Do you make good decisions?
16. What do you want most as a child? Do you get it?
17. Who loves you the most? How do they show it?
18. How do you act when you feel unloved?
19. How do you get your parents to love you?
20. What is the best way to be comforted and nurtured?
21. Do you discuss your needs, wants and desires?
22. How do you express yourself?
23. What do you not want to share?
24. What are your talents? Are they recognized and encouraged?
25. What do you want to be when you grow up?
26. What do you love to do?
27. What do you fantasize about?
28. Where do you feel most at home? Not at home?
29. Do you feel any connection to the Divine? Does it create inner peace?
30. Does Spirit communicate with you? How?

GUIDED VISUALIZATION

Find that relaxing place where you're free of distractions. Set the mood. Let your breath guide you deeper within. As you inhale, bring in calming energy and as you exhale, release any thoughts or worries.

Imagine yourself in an ancient grotto between two stone pillars. A spiral stone staircase descends down into the earth. There are lit candles on each step. You set an intention to discover lost parts of yourself. When you're ready, slowly walk down the steps. Know that with each step, you descend further into yourself. You are safe. Move downward, slowly and gently. The Guiding Power of Spirit moves with you. You are loved and protected. Let each step take you deeper within.

At the bottom of the staircase an outer chamber leads into a cave. This outer chamber allows you to stand at the threshold of your inner sanctuary. Rest for a moment and prepare for the possibilities that exist within the inner chamber. Scan your body and notice any thoughts, feelings or sensations. There may be fear or anticipation, anxiety or excitement. Accept yourself just the way you are. Allow whatever happens to happen.

When you are ready, move past the threshold and step into the inner sanctuary. Shimmering light flickers at the center of the cave. A burning fire, surrounded by a circle of stones, creates a warm, cozy atmosphere.

Find a resting place in this sanctuary. You may want to be near the fire or near the walls. Breathe in the essence of the illuminating light. It offers protection and insight. Allow the light to bathe you in a sense of well-being and love.

As you receive the light in this sanctuary, call for your orphaned parts – those parts that have been disowned, neglected, abused, lost or forgotten. Let them know they are welcome. Accept them. Love them all.

You may find one child or a collection of children. The child may be a girl or a boy, or there may be twins. If an orphan does not appear, merely allow yourself to be comforted by the light. If a child approaches, notice the dear little one looks. Ask the child's age and name.

Peer into the child's eyes. What do you see? Touch the child's heart. What do you feel? Allow any emotions to flow. The child may need or want something from you or may even show you what you need. Embrace this little child and take the dear one into your arms. Ask what the orphan needs. Listen. Be available. Connect with this child. The orphan may need safety and protection, love and security. The child may want to be seen and be heard, or to be held and comforted. Listen and accept. Allow any emotions to emerge. There's no right or wrong. Just allow, accept and love.

Cradle the child and tell the little one that you offer comfort and protection, safety and security. Begin a dialogue. You are there to listen and heal, to forgive and love. You have found your orphan. Hold the dear little soul close to your heart. Welcome the connection. Cherish your feelings. Embrace the insights.

Remain there awhile. Reclaim the lost parts of yourself. Acceptance and love provide soothing balm on the journey toward wholeness. Tell the orphan you are glad you have found your lost child. You are committed to bringing the little one home. Say that you love and accept the orphan unconditionally. Notice how your child responds.

Hug your orphan and ask if the dear little one wants to return with you. Your orphan may want to remain in the safety of the cave or the child may want to reside in your heart. Be receptive to your orphan's needs. Stay with your child for awhile.

When you're ready to return to the outer chamber and back into the present, say goodbye to the inner sanctuary. You can return whenever you wish. Bring the memory of your orphan with you as you begin the climb up the stone staircase. As you ascend each step, move slowly and gently back into your body. Feel the warmth in your heart. With each succeeding step, increase your awareness of the outside world. Continue the steady climb, upward and upward, until you reach the top. Step back into consciousness and return more fully into your body. Stretch your limbs and, when you're ready, open your eyes.

Take a moment and write about this experience in your journal.

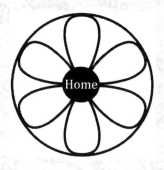

CHAPTER FOUR

WAKE-UP CALLS AND SIGNPOSTS

Awakening moves the tectonic plates of your psyche and sends

shock waves to every corner of your life, initiating a profound

transformation at the core of your being.

– Stephan Bodian

When I lived in Australia, the peculiar call of the kookaburra woke me each morning. Its rat-a-tat koo-koo-koo-koo-koo-ka-ka-ka-ka-ka sounded like raucous laughter. According to Aboriginal legend, the bird's rollicking laugh was created to wake humans from their dreams and signal the start of a new day. Since the kookaburra called the dawn, it was, in effect, an alarm clock without a snooze button. It became my symbol for wake-up calls that stop us in our tracks when we've strayed from our homeward path.

In the previous chapter I discussed the orphan state where, disconnected from our True Self, we have wandered far away from Home. As we walk in darkness, we replay old video clips that reinforce the trance of separation. As orphans, we're unaware of our beliefs and behavioral patterns, our many choices, the interconnection of life, and the Guiding Power of Spirit. Fortunately, our GPS beams a ray of light to wake us up and illuminate signposts to guide us back Home.

My early morning awakenings began with my grandmother. She had worked on a farm in Poland, and even after she migrated to America, she would rise at the crack of dawn. She lived in the basement apartment below and would wake my mother at five in the morning to get her out the door by 5:30 a.m. so she wouldn't be late for her job at Campbell's Soup. My grandmother's alarm was a carnival cane that she banged against the low ceiling. My mother would stamp her foot on the floor and signal she was up and running.

After my mother left for work, my siblings and I were next in line. Following our mother's example, we would dutifully stomp our feet whenever we heard my grandmother's call. If my grandmother didn't hear our hoof beats tromping overhead, she would employ the cane again. If we ignored the rapping and slept in, she would make a grand appearance and get us really moving!

Wake-up calls do just that. They draw our attention to reconnect with one or more of our six vehicles so we can move along the path of transformation. We may be called to take better care of the physical home of the body or we may be reminded to eliminate negative toxicity in the emotional home. We may be asked to clear the mind when it houses negative chatter or we may be guided to remove anger and resentment in relationships so we can love more freely. Our inner voice may direct us to reduce inhibitions and speak our truth or we may be instructed to see life through forgiving eyes as we create a vision aligned with Spirit.

Wake-up calls are meant to expand our consciousness away from ego toward our True Self. They highlight the fact that we don't know what we're meant to know and point us in a direction to uncover the truth. Wake-up calls often begin as gentle reminders. If we remain fast asleep and rush around with frenetic lives and mental chatter, we don't hear the loving tap to get us moving. When we don't respond to a call, and bury our head under blankets, messages are sent in increasingly dramatic fashion, such as traumas and personal crises. A partner may walk out, a life-threatening illness may strike, anxiety or despair may set in or career and finances may be lost. Not surprisingly, when the pain of living becomes greater than the pain of change, we become motivated to change.

Crises generate heat for transformation. Our inner GPS employs a principle of thermodynamics. The Greek word for heat is *therme* while *dynamis* means power. Thermodynamics is the study of heat and its ability to bring about change. Consider the Australian banksia tree. It produces a hard nut, the size of a large pine cone. To stimulate regeneration, the nut requires intense heat from a forest fire to release its seeds. No fire, no new trees.

The same principle applies to us. No wake-up calls, no transformation. Internal conflict creates dynamic heat. The energy cracks the window of an unconscious mind. Traumas open fissures in our psyche so eyes can turn inward, past the ruins of archaic beliefs toward the beckoning heart of authentic connection. In essence, the hero or heroine receives a call to adventure. Epic stories portray such individuals who right a wrong, accomplish amazing feats, discover true love, battle inner demons or radically change their lives. Should they fail to answer the call, they risk falling into a deeper hole of unconsciousness where they remain until the next crisis. Those come as bolts of lightening.

In July of 2004, I received one such call at two in the morning. My daughter, Melissa, phoned me from a hospital bed in Thailand. While she was riding on the back of a motorcycle on a rainy day, the bike had skidded on a bend in the highway. She was thrown to the pavement and hit by an oncoming car. Her hand was severely mangled. Her mother and I flew to Thailand and arranged for Melissa to return to Chicago for multiple surgeries to repair lost tendons. Her hand thankfully mended, but not before turning her life and several others' lives upside down.

At the time, I had a comfortable life with a private practice, scheduled time for writing, a lovely condo that overlooked a small lake in a Chicago suburb and a group of wonderful friends. But something was missing. I had fallen asleep again and was meandering through life.

My daughter's wake-up call propelled me into a maelstrom. Knowing that I could have lost my daughter, I returned from Thailand with a burning desire to reignite the fire in my belly. I reviewed the facets of my life and took action. I joined a health club, signed up for yoga classes and personal growth seminars, shifted relationships, altered my attitude, and formulated a plan to relocate to California, which had been beckoning me for some time. Though I had traveled on and off the spiritual path through-out my life, my daughter's accident acted like a scorching forest fire that released the seed for a passionate embrace of the journey back Home. I have been committed to that path ever since.

Interestingly, Melissa's accident became her own wake-up call. It thrust her onto a course that led her to Australia to complete a nursing degree and a career path to help others. Not surprisingly, her injury created ripples among friends and family. Crises offer poignant moments for reflection and evaluation.

Such incidents jolt one out of a programmed mindset. In the Bible, Paul had his "Road to Damascus" conversion after he was blinded by the light. Epiphanies are meant to restore vision. Those who've experienced life-altering episodes undergo radical change. Such episodes often deepen a spiritual life, strengthen loving rela-tionships, and spur a renewed mission or purpose for living.

I have witnessed many of my clients' wake-up calls. More often than not, they had repeatedly pushed the snooze button whenever they heard the alarm and sought help only after a series of crises. A woman with breast cancer was called to shift her focus away from helping others toward healing herself. A husband who was served divorce papers came to the realization that his marriage was more important than golf or his job. An addicted adolescent had to break through denial and enter a recovery program.

The purpose of the wake-up call is to grab our attention and stir us toward action. The significant event begins a transformational arc. Prior to the call, we roam aimlessly as an orphan, oblivious to our True Self. The wake-up call forces us to realize we're lost and in need of a map. If we refuse to stop for directions, we slip into denial, avoidance or fear, and we fall back to sleep. Those with self-destructive habits or in dysfunctional relationships receive count-less wake-up calls before they crash at the bottom and hear the gong of truth.

Be assured that messages from the GPS remain constant. They continually instruct us to recognize our lost way and alter our thoughts and behaviors. Once we courageously steer our vehicles toward Home, transformation accelerates and signposts readily appear.

To understand signposts, consider the Global Positioning Sys-tem in a car. When the receiver is turned on, one is guided toward a destination. If the driver makes a wrong turn, s/he is rerouted to get back on course. The same concept applies to our internal GPS. It signals when we have veered off our path and then navigates us back Home – if we pay attention.

In *The Secret Language of Signs,* Denise Linn states that signs have two functions. "They serve as messengers of important information about your present circumstances and even about your future and they act as reflections of where you are in your life."[1] In essence, they stand out as signposts to point you in the right direction.

When I was a boy, I received a Christmas gift from my younger sister, Rita. She was excited about handing me the present. I was excited too, until I opened the gift. I found three pencils, an eraser and three comic books. I immediately checked the present she had given my brother. His gift, a set of screwdrivers, seemed far better than mine, so I ungratefully grumbled about my sister's choice of presents. She was crestfallen.

I continued to receive pens and pencil sets over the years from many people, and finally stopped complaining once I realized that the GPS had been relentlessly telling me to write. If I had grasped that insight as a young boy, I could have embraced my sister's gift with appreciation and love.

If we don't have the maturity and wisdom to recognize signposts at the time, we can discover the markers laid out on our journey when we later review our life. The threads of connection may have offered lessons or prepared us for a career path, a relationship journey, or a spiritual odyssey. Using hindsight, we can gain insight about our unfolding story and understand the symbols that guide us into uncharted territory.

Similar to markers on a highway, signposts steer us through the dense fog of the material world. Some signs tell us when we're lost; others let us know we're on the right road. Some caution us about construction sites; others offer an alternative route. By paying attention, we negotiate around problems. It's when we lose our focus that we end up in a ditch or off a cliff.

Signposts can show up when we least expect and may serendipitously appear in symbols, words, animals, nature or dreams. In fact, signs occur every day. A phone call from a friend, an inspirational message on the radio, a poignant email, or an intuitive flash may guide us to slow down, pay attention, and attend to an important matter of the day. We may be guided to forgive some-one, repair or leave a loveless relationship, take a risk, or alter our attitude.

Signs act like a car's warning system. Red lights on the dash-board appear when the gas tank is near empty, seat belts aren't buckled, or the car needs service. We understand their function and don't become unduly alarmed. Once they have our attention, we know what to do. However, if we used duct tape to block out those irritating red lights, our car would eventually grind to a halt. And we might complain about the negligent manufacturer!

Like the car's sensors, our body uses pain and discomfort to alert us to problems. We may be directed to visit a dentist or other practitioner and have a malady be diagnosed and treated. When we don't listen to our body, symptoms intensify until we take action.

Louise Hay, in her seminal book *You Can Heal Your Life,* re-ferred to negative mental patterns in the body as "dis-ease." She wrote that since thoughts create illness, thoughts can also heal. "The body, like everything else in life, is a mirror of our inner thoughts and beliefs."[2]

After my father deserted the family, I developed a severe case of eczema. My mother took me to several doctors who tried to treat the angry wounds with ointments. None seemed effective. Of course, no one asked me if I was angry, sad or frightened. The infected areas were obviously screaming for help. The skin even-tually healed when the environment became safe once again. My mother found a cream that helped, though I now believe it was the loving application of the balm that produced the cure. To this day, my skin remains a loving messenger. Minor flare-ups occur when-ever I neglect the signals from my body for balance and self-care.

It's often easier to notice physical sensations that demand at-tention. However, we can also expand our awareness to the rich array of messages that emanate from feelings, thoughts, relation-ships, sounds and sights. They instruct us and, when necessary, flash alerts to take action. Such poignant moments create the feel-ing of déjà vu or send shivers pulsating down the spine.

Our consciousness interfaces our internal and external worlds, which resonate like tuning forks. In the law of attraction, we at-tract what we are and see what we think. The outer world becomes a projective screen for our mind. Therefore, if we repeatedly hear or spot a certain message, it may be that a signpost is calling our attention. For example, if the word "warrior" stands out repeatedly in the newspaper, on the radio or TV, or in casual conversations, and there is an emotional resonance, we may be called to act like a warrior. This may mean adopting a more disciplined life or battling through adversity.

When a signpost reveals itself, it requires self-reflection, knowledge and insight to decipher its meaning. Money often symbolizes energy, colors indicate different emotional states, and animals represent different attributes of the personality. While there are numerous compendiums on symbols and their translations, it's important to discover the unique meaning of our personal signposts.

Signs often appear in clusters. The psychiatrist Carl Jung introduced the word "synchronicity" to define two or more events, similar in nature, that were meaningfully connected with no apparent cause or effect.[3] Synchronicity time- stamps as interrelated significant moments that need attention.

When I lived in Australia, there was a period of time when I kept spotting "Smash Repair" signs. This was the Aussie term for car repairs. It seemed that everywhere I went, day after day, I saw billboards of car wrecks or dented cars on the road. During this period, I picked up a hitch-hiker, something I rarely did. But I had this intuition to stop for him. While in the car, the man told me he worked at a smash repair shop. After I dropped him off, I drove to the office and parked my car. As soon as I entered the building, I heard screeching tires outside and a loud bang. Two cars had collided. The accident sent another smashing message.

When I pondered the meaning, I recognized that I was holding onto considerable anger. It was clear to me that unless I cleared out my anger, I'd end up in a crash. Not surprisingly, all the clients I saw that day dealt with issues of anger. At first I thought it was my projection but, before I could say hello, client after client launched into angry outbursts about their situations. Since therapists reflect back what we most need to hear, I listened attentively to my own advice. Release the anger and practice forgiveness. I tried practicing what I preached, and as I did, the external images of smashing cars faded. However, a month later, I was parked at a restaurant and a car pulled out and dented my door. I obviously needed more practice at forgiveness.

Since many of us live in an urban setting, signposts tend to reflect that world. However, animals and nature provide a rich medium of symbols. Indigenous people, intimately connected with their environment, read the rhythm of their surroundings to gather food and set up camp. The Aborigines in Australia developed legends about celestial systems, earth formations, creatures and plants, and looked to them for signs in their daily lives. As mentioned earlier, the laughter of the kookaburra woke humans from their dreams.

Bob Randall, an Aboriginal elder, described signposts in his book *Songman.* "We were continually being given information about our environment through these creation stories. . . we grew up with the knowledge that everything in nature was part of our family. They taught us how to track for food. We learned how to judge the freshness of the tracks we found so that we would know if an animal was still around or if we were wasting our time. . . . The land contours gave us information about foods that were available in a particular area."[4]

Unfortunately, many of us have lost that intimate connection with the land. I suspect that the longing for nature propels people to connect with the animal kingdom through pets. Not surprisingly, pet owners establish a special bond with their dogs, cats and other animals and communicate with them on an intuitive level. Pets often provide wake-up calls every morning to get going. No doubt, we've all heard inspirational stories of pets lifting spirits, teaching lessons, warning about potential danger, and saving lives.

My dear friend, Audrey Jones, has a little poodle named Silver. Audrey is a psychologist in Australia and conducts therapy with Silver at her side. When clients get upset, the poodle uncannily offers them one of her soft toys and looks at them through caring eyes, like any good therapist. The clients notice Silver's attentiveness and are touched by the loving act of kindness.

Clearly, signs appear in numerous forms, from the animate to the inanimate. One final area worth mentioning is the world of dreams. They offer an amazing font of wisdom. Unfortunately, many people view dreams as weird and discount this universal phenomenon as flotsam and jetsam. Since our critical, judgmental

minds often block vital information from reaching our consciousness, dreams offer yet another vehicle for our GPS to transmit
messages.

I have recorded my dreams for over 30 years, have participated
in dream groups, and have listened to countless dreams reported
by clients. As a result, I have a deep appreciation of the dreaming
process and the wealth of untapped knowledge.

The language of dreams is symbols, images and emotions. Similar to any other language, it requires study and practice to correctly interpret meaning. While there are many different theories
about dream interpretation, my personal belief is that dreams not
only provide insight but are also a call to action.

One of the earliest examples of this process is recorded in the
Book of Genesis.[5] The Pharaoh told Joseph that he dreamed he
was standing by the river Nile and saw seven fat cows that were eat-
en by seven lean cows. In a second dream he saw seven ears of ripe
corn swallowed by seven ears of withered corn. Joseph correctly
interpreted the dream and said that seven years of bounty would
be followed by seven years of famine. In addition, he clarified the
call to action, namely that Pharaoh should store the excess food
during the bountiful years and prepare for seven lean years.

We can all be like Joseph and interpret our dreams. They are
road signs that appear in the early morning mist of our minds.
They beckon us forward on our transpersonal journey. To decode
the symbols and stay the course, here are five simple steps:

1. Become Conscious of Your Dreams

Keep a journal by the bed and record dreams as soon as you
wake up. If you can't recall your dreams, program your mind the
night before with the intention that you want to remember them.
Be patient while you prime the dreaming pump with your conscious intention. When the dreams arrive, write without judgment
or analysis. This can be difficult because most people want to
quickly analyze or erase a disturbing image. All dreams, including
the bizarre and the exotic, can offer profound messages.

The true challenge in this step is to muster the courage to write
freely without censoring thoughts. It's natural to want only happy,
beautiful dreams. If an ugly scene appears, the immediate impulse

is to suppress the image. Therefore, it's crucial that you give your-self permission to record your dreams without judgment. A jour-nal should be for your eyes only. Sharing with others prematurely will inhibit self-expression. Once you are comfortable with your dreaming process, you can share it with those who are open, re-ceptive and encouraging.

Since I can be fairly analytic, I avoided interpreting my dreams during my first year of journaling. Back then, I had to practice let-ting go of what was supposedly appropriate in dreams. Actually, everything is appropriate. After all, it's only a dream!

You may ask, "What if I conjure up murderous scenes or weird sexual escapades?" Again, don't be alarmed. You may be called to bring into the light unconsciously suppressed material. Remem-ber, your GPS wants to grab your attention. Graphic, juicy symbols are sure ways to do that.

2. List the Symbols, Images and Emotions

During this second step, objectively record the symbols, images and emotional states. Dream symbols interact with one another to create moving images. We saw this clearly in the dream that Joseph translated. Lean cows ate fattened cows; withered ears of corn consumed ripe ones. In addition to symbols, dreams convey an emotional state. The Pharaoh felt so disturbed about the im-ages that he summoned Joseph.

Each symbol and emotional state is highly significant. Some dreams will have only a few; others will play out like a full-length movie. Alter any of them and the meaning shifts. Imagine a grief-stricken couple standing by a grave. Shift a symbol, such as the grave to a wedding, or the emotional state, from grief to joy, and you'll have a completely different scenario and interpretation. Therefore, focus on the symbols and emotions that appear in your dream.

Here is an example of one of my journal entries after I moved back to Chicago after living in sunny Australia.

I peer at a ten-gallon fish tank. The water is cloudy and murky. Color-ful fish are sluggish and at risk of dying because of all the excrement. The filter is clogged and needs to be changed. I remove the plastic filter and take out the clogged fibers that were once white but are now filthy black. I siphon out the sediment from the bottom of the tank and add fresh water.

The dream contains numerous symbols: small tank, colorful fish, murky water, death, excrement, clogged filter, white into black, siphon, bottom, sediment, and fresh water. The dream evoked emotions of lethargy, dread and fear of loss.

Most people stop the dreaming process after they identify the symbols. Insightful gifts arrive when we work with them. That takes us to the next step.

3. Associate the Symbols, Images and Feelings to Your Life.

The next step is to use the dream as a projective device for your current life. Dreams often hold symbols from our childhood or from recent events. A movie could act as a trigger for the psyche. So imagine yourself as a writer. Weave the symbols and emotions into a story with you as the main character. Be creative and expressive as you associate the images with your life. Don't look for the "right" interpretation. Rather, look for meanings that resonate. You could begin with the sentence, "If the dream represented an aspect of my life, it would mean that . . ."

In my example, I easily related to the symbols because I once had two five-gallon fish tanks. The dream occurred during a dreary, frigid winter in Chicago. I felt depressed about the change in climate and environment. I had stopped exercising and felt cooped up indoors. I felt like the sluggish fish in the confined tank. I harbored a lot of crappy feelings about the move to Chicago. My angry emotions were clogging my life. The dream called me to siphon out the crap and the murky water (emotions are often symbolized as water). If I didn't release the toxic waste and add a fresh emotional perspective, my dream warned me that I would wallow in negative feelings.

Another of my dreams occurred when a relationship was ending. I woke up with the image of two ships that were once lashed together, separating and heading for different ports. The dream clearly represented two people heading off in different directions.

The meaning of some dreams will unfold simply as you jot them down. Others will require more thought. With practice and an increased familiarity with the symbols, you will expand your understanding of the dreaming process. While there are a number of books that provide explanations of dream symbols, the final interpretation should resonate with you as the dreamer.

4. Identify the Call to Action.

Within each dream is a kernel of advice. As you clarify the dream's message, you recognize the call to action. It may direct you to care for your body, release your emotions, shift your thoughts, work on a relationship, express your truth, or respond to a problem.

A client's dream about being speechless gave her the message to find her voice. My dream called me to siphon out the anger, practice forgiveness, get back to swimming at the health club, and create more purpose and joy in my life. Joseph offered the Pharaoh a concrete plan: choose a governor over the land, impose a tax, and store excess food during the bountiful years.

Not all dreams provide such clear answers. Sometimes the call to action becomes apparent later with an "aha" experience. If the dream is particularly troubling or complex and you have no idea what it means, consider sharing it with a trusted friend or some-one who works with dreams. An outside perspective can illuminate dark, puzzling images.

5. Follow the Wisdom of Your Dream.

Once we understand the call to action, the last step is to follow the wisdom.

When I discussed this chapter with Bonnie, a friend of mine, she described a significant dream she once had about a snake en-tering her vagina. In the dream she tugged at the snake's tail and pulled it out. She realized that it meant that the man she was dat-ing at the time was a snake in the grass. The dream's call to action was to pull him out of her life. She followed the wisdom and had no regrets, for she later married the man of her dreams.

Though my friend recognized the message of her dream, oth-ers may resist implementing the call to action. Procrastination is a form of resistance. And we now know that if we avoid following through on taking action, we'll eventually get another wake-up call. So whether the message is to take immediate action or plan for the long term, let the Guiding Power of Spirit direct you.

One final note. Some dreams can be precognitive and portend a coming event. In those situations we may be forewarned in order to be mentally prepared for a future event.

Recall my daughter's motorcycle accident. Several weeks prior to the incident, I woke in the middle of the night with an image of her wounded body lying beside a highway. I thought she was dead and rushed to her aid. In the dream she was alive but badly injured. My emotions were so intense that I awoke screaming, tears streaming down my cheeks. I felt compelled to immediately record the dream and ponder the meaning. My daughter was traveling in Asia at the time and my son and I had contemplated meeting her in Malaysia for a summer vacation. I wondered whether the dream meant I should contact my daughter and warn her to be careful or whether I was called to finalize the trip. The image of her lying on the pavement made me do both. Later, when I received that horrific phone call from the hospital in Thailand, I flashed to the dream. I had been forewarned.

Not all dreams bode ill fortune. Dreams can offer positive messages about career, prosperity, health, marriage, family and common day problems. Dreams are but one way to access inner wisdom. If you're not comfortable with dream work or journaling, look for other ways to receive messages from your GPS.

For Chuck Miller, sailing is a spiritual experience. Since he lives on his 45-foot sailboat in Long Beach, California, he must keep a sharp lookout for signposts to guide him safely back to harbor. When he sails on the open ocean, he pays attention to wind direction, weather conditions for approaching storms, passing boats or objects, and shore depth, to name a few. While at sea, he is struck by those "magical signs" such as dolphins playing in the boat's wake, beautiful sunsets, and perfect wind conditions that create a sense of awe and take him back Home.

As with Chuck, many of our signposts may be particular to our occupation or life experience. With increased awareness, we can recognize their significance. On the other hand, if we can't spot the signs, it may mean there isn't enough light. Every day the Earth revolves around the sun and moves into darkness, but the sun's light reflects off the moon in the evening sky. Even in our bleakest moments, the Guiding Power of Spirit pierces the dark night with a glimmer of hope. It merely requires trust that the All-Knowing Source guides us at the right moment past the traffic jams onto that well-lit highway.

We will inevitably make a wrong turn or not answer a call. Relationships, work, family and finances continually draw our attention. Fortunately, if we miss an exit, we are given other chances. All it takes is the realization that we have driven off course. By acknowledging that we have fallen asleep, we wake up once again ready to spot the signposts. We return to the journey with a greater commitment, and that takes us to the next stage – **Staying Awake**.

MAPPING EXERCISE

Set aside 15-30 minutes for this exercise. Create a lifeline that covers your journey, from birth until the present. As you plot the map, notice the patterns. They foreshadow your future unless you create a new map. That comes in a subsequent chapter.

On a large sheet of paper, draw a horizontal line across the middle. On the far left, mark the date you were born, and at the far right mark today's date and your current age. To the extreme left, draw a vertical line that intersects the horizontal line. Number this line zero to five above the horizontal line and zero to minus five below the line.

LIFELINE

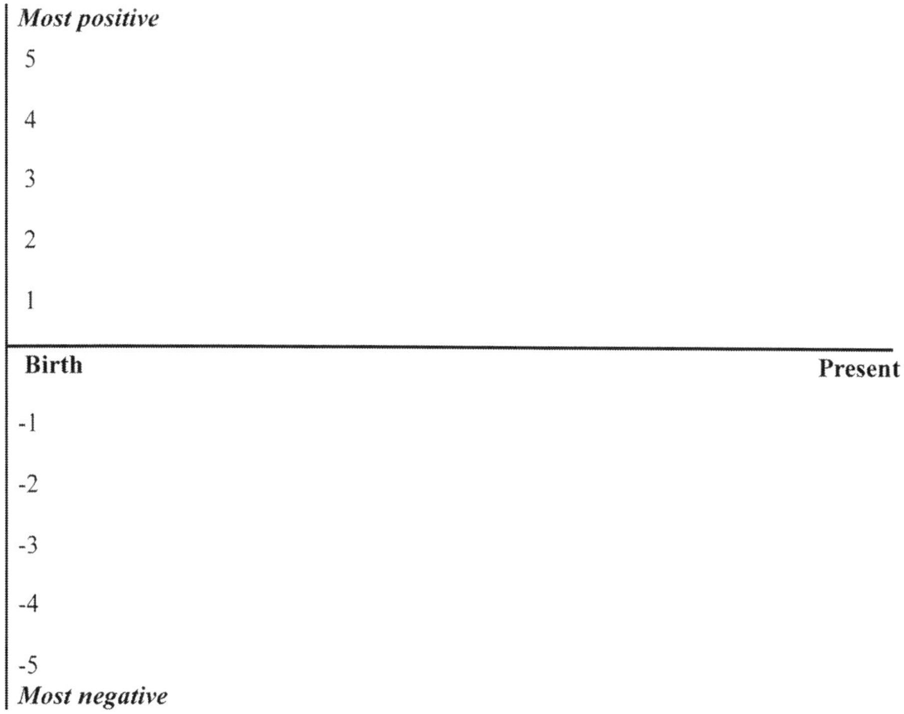

Most positive

5

4

3

2

1

Birth   **Present**

-1

-2

-3

-4

-5

Most negative

Write the significant events in your life, both positive and negative, from birth to the present, on the horizontal line. Record the events by chronological age and/or year. Include the major developmental stages such as pre-school, adolescence, menstruation, first sexual experience, marriage, etc.

If an incident was positive, expansive, or connecting to your True Self, mark an "X" **above** "the event" using the scale of 1-5, with 5 indicating the most positive experience. For incidents that were negative or disconnecting from Self, mark an "X" from -1 to -5 **below** the horizontal line, with -5 as the most negative. This lifeline will distinguish the uplifting "mountain" experiences above the horizontal line from your "down in the valley" moments.

Notice the empty spaces where there were neither positive nor negative events or your memory was blocked. If you can't recall key periods of your life, don't become alarmed. The gaps show the times when you were asleep. As you awaken, you may recall painful moments such as abuse or neglect. You may also discover signposts or guides that led you out of darkness. If some recollections become overly disturbing, distance yourself from the emotions by imagining you are watching your life from behind a one-way mirror where you are safe and protected. From that position, you can watch the drama of your life unfold without the overwhelming emotions.

Once you've completed the lifeline, ask yourself these questions:

- Are there more uplifting or painful experiences?
- Can you identify any life patterns?
- Can you recognize the wake-up calls?
- How did you answer them?
- When you pressed the snooze button, what did you do?
- What are the lessons and themes of your life?
- Do they get repeated?
- Did major crises teach you any lessons? (For example, the death of a loved one can teach about embracing the present with gratitude.)
- What is your current wake-up call?
- What is its call to action?
- What are the obstacles and challenges?
- Where is your roadmap heading?

Now let's examine the signposts on your lifeline.

Symbols often trigger a heightened awareness that breaks us out of a sleepwalking trance back into conscious alignment with our Home Base. A symbol operates like a pre-set button on a radio that locks onto a signal. It may be a number, word or phrase, special song, animal or object.

- Identify the signs or symbols that marked any turning points.
- Are there recurrent signposts?
- Does any symbol have a special meaning?
- What is its message?
- Is there a symbol that connects you with the Guiding Power of Spirit?
- How can you use that signpost in your life now?

GUIDED VISUALIZATION

Once you make yourself comfortable, let gentle breathing relax your body and calm your mind.

Now imagine that you're at a movie theater. The room darkens and images flicker on the screen. You're about to watch the film of your life. Let all of your senses create a three-dimensional picture. The movie opens in present time. It shows you calmly practicing a visualization exercise. You notice that, rather than playing forward, the scenes slowly move backward in time. Sitting safely in the theater, you view your life with objectivity and wonder as it continues to play backwards. It stops at special events or stages of your life. You watch yourself morph into a younger you. You notice your relationships with others and the lessons they offer. You can pause along the way as you see yourself as a young adult, then as an adolescent. You view yourself as a pre-teen and younger child. The movie plays all the way back to your birth. You watch your delivery.

You then move back into the uterus where you float peacefully. You move further back in time to the point of conception. You take another leap backward when you are but a soul, a being of light, connected with All That Is. Pause for a moment and enjoy the scene. You are bathed in radiant light, connected to the Guiding Power of Spirit. Feel the unconditional love permeating your very essence. Feel the deep connection with your True Self.

Now imagine that you receive a message to enter the material world. You are called to have an amazing adventure with new experiences, lessons and relationships. You willingly accept the call and move forward in time. As a being of light, you take on human form. Hold the image of your bright soul as you watch yourself grow and develop. There may be events that cause forgetfulness but there are incidents or wake-up calls that trigger an awareness of the loving light within. As you move forward in time, watch your story unfold. Notice the times when your light shined bright and the times when it dimmed. Each moment brought many lessons. Notice the signposts along the way. They help you remember your True Self. Notice that the light is always there, waiting for you to come Home.

Continue your forward journey until you see yourself in present time. Now ask the Guiding Power of Spirit for a symbol to help you remember your very essence. The symbol will act as a signpost on your continuing journey. Ask for the symbol. It may be a song, a word, a number or an object. Whenever that symbol appears, it will act as a trigger to remind you to stay awake. If a symbol doesn't appear, don't worry. It will reveal itself to you in the perfect time and place.

Now see an imaginary clock ticking slowly. The clock reminds you to move back into present time. Let the ticking clock gently bring you back to your body and your surrounding environment. Take a deep breath and exhale. Continue your conscious breathing. You feel refreshed and rejuvenated, ready to continue with the rest of your day.

Take a moment to record any thoughts and feelings. Draw a picture of any symbol you received. If one hasn't appeared, don't worry. It'll come when you're ready. Congratulate yourself for having the courage to view a map of your life.

CHAPTER FIVE

STAYING AWAKE

Who looks outside, dreams; who looks inside, awakens.

– C.G. Jung

Over 20 years ago when I lived in Sydney, I attended a series of meditation classes. After a Sunday intensive of blissful meditation, I returned to my car at 9:30 at night, ready for the 30-minute drive home. I was in an extremely relaxed state with an open mind. I started the engine and received an intuitive message to take a specific route. My judgmental mind hadn't yet kicked into its habitual chattering, so I complied with the request. As I drove, I received further guidance. Actually, it was a series of instructions to alter my course with occasional right and left turns.

After 20 minutes, I became impatient and wondered how long the journey would continue. The internal message immediately replied, "You're almost there." When I approached a two-story red brick house, I was told to slow down and park near the building. I made several U-turns to verify I was in the right place, and each time I drove past the house the message was clear – that was the building. Though I was still in a relaxed zone, I became nervous when, after I parked across the street, the internal voice instructed me, "Talk to the people in the house." My judgmental mind immediately responded, "No way!"

As soon as those words entered my mind, however, a young couple stepped out the front door and walked to their car parked near the building.

The voice calmly said, "They are the ones. Talk to them."

I argued back, "What the hell am I supposed to say? That a strange voice asked me to come and speak with you?"

At the time, I worked at a child and adolescent psychiatry department. I wondered how I'd respond to a patient who told me about hearing internal voices instructing him to talk with strangers. My clinical mind took control. I folded my arms tightly around my chest in an act of resistance and refused to budge. I was not about to talk with anyone. However, I remained in my car to watch the unfolding episode.

As it turned out, the couple had a long discussion by their car. The man lifted the hood and fiddled near the engine. After he shut the hood, the couple talked further. Meanwhile, I kept receiving internal nudges to speak with them. That evening my resistance won out. The couple eventually entered their car and drove away. I exhaled a sigh of relief. Then I realized that fear had prevented some holy encounter. Though I had experienced an awakening during the meditation, I had become paralyzed by fear and had fallen back asleep.

During the following week, I pondered that incident with great disappointment. I was upset with myself for not having the courage to follow my internal guidance. I also realized how difficult it was to stay awake. Fortunately, lessons repeat themselves until they are learned.

Several weeks later I took a train to work. When a well-dressed man in a gray suit sat next to me, I received another intuitive message, "Speak to him." I initially resisted but, remembering the previous lost opportunity, I asked silently, "Can you give me some help?"

No sooner did I hold that thought when the man casually asked if there was anything interesting in the Sydney Morning Herald that I held on my lap. That provided an opening. Before long, our conversation moved to meditation. As it turned out, the man was adept at a particular method of stilling the mind. After sharing his techniques, he confided that he was instructed to talk with me. I realized then that all of us receive some form of guidance. Yet we often don't act on it because of fear. Then later we feel disappointment.

My encounters in Sydney taught me a crucial lesson. My internal GPS was available all the time. However, I had to stay awake and overcome my fears and constricting beliefs. I strengthened my trust in Spirit through trial and error, success and disappointment. The act of not following my GPS taught me about missed opportunities and ignited the desire to take greater risks and listen to the intuitive messages. Connected with my GPS, I knew that I would meet the right people at the right time for meaningful exchanges. But this required me to stay awake.

Staying awake is about increasing awareness so we can discover that we've been asleep and that we don't know what we need to know. What we will know is that there's something far better than the dream state. We will also recognize that guidance is available. We may not know how to access our GPS, but we can become more receptive to the light. We may initially squint at the brightness of day but as we get used to the light we realize that if we don't remain awake at the wheel, we'll hit another crisis or, at the very least, return back to well-worn habitual paths.

An awakened state heightens awareness of sensations, feelings, thoughts, relationships, communication and perceptions. Strangely, as we stay awake, we may find our lives getting worse. When we're asleep, we become unconscious about the pain in our lives, but as we awaken, we become acutely aware of the thought patterns, feelings and behaviors that cause us to numb-out, flee from problems, or aggressively satisfy cravings.

Imagine sitting on the floor in a half-lotus position. If, after awhile, your legs have fallen asleep, you would stretch to increase circulation. The sensation of "pins and needles" would ripple through your legs. This represents an example of awakening. As awareness circulates through your life, you become more conscious about being out of alignment with your True Self. As Eckhart Tolle states, "The essential part of the awakening is the recognition of the unawakened you . . ."[1]

This may be especially disconcerting when we feel the "pins and needles." Some may experience "sharp nails and broken glass." During this phase, we may become overwhelmed while the fog lifts. Discomfort and pain, terror and disbelief, grief and self-pity, anger and blame are some of the feelings that may arise during this process. We may become frightened of losing our identity and cherished beliefs or upset that we have lost our Home. We may be tempted to avoid the pain, pull the covers over our head, and go back to sleep.

It's as if we are driving along the coast while passing through a fog. We follow a bend in the road and the sun pierces the sky. We catch a glimpse of the beautiful countryside before we drive back into the mist. The transitions in and out of the fog provide contrasts between sleep time and wake time. Acceptance of our current state, no matter what it is, allows us to receive the light and move past our fears.

To put the stage of Staying Awake in perspective, let's cast the initial phase of Adaptation as starting our descent down a steep mountain. The Orphan stage takes us downward to the further-most point away from Home into the valley of darkness. The Wake-up calls break us out of our slumber while the Signposts point the way toward the mountain. Staying awake now asks that we prepare for the climb even when dark clouds impede our visibility. This is a time to face insecurity and fear. We may doubt whether we have the strength to complete what appears to be a daunting journey. To some, the mountain peak will look tantalizingly close. They'll want to rush to enlightenment without appreciating that they need provisions, tools, companions, a map and a guide. As soon as they start the journey, they'll become overwhelmed and give up. Staying awake requires commitment and effort. It's about building a foundation before the climb.

As we awaken to the Guiding Power of Spirit, we will gather the courage to remain steadfast against the temptation to retreat into sleepy habits. This is a time to evaluate what we want to take with us and what we want to leave behind. This can be challenging for relationships, especially if one partner wants to stay awake and the other wants to slumber. The temptation for the one awaken-ing is to expend considerable energy stirring the other. This often leads to anger, blame and frustration on both parts. It's far better for one to focus on getting clarity about one's own journey and then extending an invitation to a partner who, hopefully, accepts the Wake-up call. Two awakened souls traveling together can be a blessed event. However, two souls at different stages of development may be compelled to part ways. Acceptance, forgiveness and love are the tools to deal with any ruptures. No matter the circumstances, anyone can still climb out of bed and walk toward the light.

As the fog of illusions fade, we experience a spiritual rebirth. The Guiding Power of Spirit expands consciousness into the six vehicles. The light of awareness illuminates the body, emotions, thoughts, relationships, communication and perceptions. We may cringe at the sight of our constrictions, negative thoughts and behaviors. However, we must persevere through the discomfort as we prepare for the climb up the mountain.

The fog will return and resurrect our fears. They are merely projections. They block our communication with our GPS. If our parents were over-controlling, domineering or punished us severely, those internal images will be projected toward the Divine. We might fear retribution and damnation from a wrathful Supreme Being and expect to receive judgment and punishment. The paradigm of a God of wrath merely represents a downloaded program.

Staying awake moves us beyond those beliefs. We can hear the loving voice of Spirit instead of the terrifying messages of hell and damnation. When grace illuminates our lives, we see past the "false self" that is based on fear and perceive our "True Self" based on love.

During those awakened moments, we step out of the fog and witness, firsthand, the truth of John Newton's memorable lyrics: "Amazing Grace, how sweet the sound, that saved a wretch like me! I once was lost, but now am found; was blind, but now I see."

The GPS provides the amazing grace to remove the cataracts of illusion. The flashes of clarity reveal disconnections, lessons for learning, opportunities for growth, and awareness of our spiritual nature. We then see our sacred journey. However, once we step onto the path, there's no turning back. The hero and heroine who answer the call must leave the familiar world and pass through a threshold, symbolizing transition from one realm to another.

In *The Wizard of Oz,* Dorothy is transported from Kansas to an extraordinary world. Her awakening begins as she steps with both trepidation and excitement onto the yellow brick road. In her transformational adventure she discovers characters that represent the quest for mind, heart and courage. Like Dorothy, we must embrace those qualities, face adversity, and discover our purpose as we overcome our deepest fears and awaken to the realization that there's no place like Home.

Awakening to Home asks that we pay attention. This requires us to be mindful of the present even when our lives are unbalanced. The Buddhist monk Thich Nhat Hanh describes this practice of mindfulness as ". . . a kind of light that shines upon all your thoughts, all your feelings, all your actions, and all your words."[2]

When we pay attention, we slow down the whirling propellers of our internal chatter and recognize our senses, feelings and thoughts. We notice how we relate and communicate. We become aware of our perceptions. We become present with whatever is – a major step toward mastering life and embracing inner peace. Though we may be uncomfortable with our transparency, we experience relief when we recognize the truth.

We don't have to join a monastery or spend hours in a meditation group to practice being mindful. We can achieve moments of peace while washing dishes, mowing the lawn, shoveling snow, exercising, playing with children, talking with family, or typing on the computer. All it requires is a moment-to-moment consciousness.

Having said that, mindfulness is not an easy practice, especially when we step onto the moving walkway of life. I can attest to the fact that I have no problem worrying. That comes easily. To achieve inner peace I have to continually practice staying awake. When I forget, help appears unexpectedly.

I recently woke up at 2 a.m. after hearing my neighbor's boisterous voice. Living one floor below me, he was engrossed in a loud phone conversation that spilled through his open window. There was no going back to sleep, even with ear plugs. I eventually climbed out of my bed to complain when my neighbor abruptly ended the phone conversation. Unfortunately, I couldn't get back to sleep. So with my eyes wide open, I pondered the meaning of this rude awakening. As it so happened, I was editing this chapter on staying awake. I couldn't help but notice the Universe's joke – at my expense.

Sometimes awakening is like that. We may be fast asleep and even immersed in a wonderful dream when an incident wakes us up. We may recognize that we're running ourselves ragged, that we're involved in an unhealthy relationship, or not taking care of ourselves. Once we become aware of the situation, we often feel a sense of relief that we're honestly facing it.

In the situation with my neighbor, I recognized that I was burning the candle at both ends and was disconnected from my body. I needed to slow down and get some rest. Ironically, I had to lose a night's sleep to achieve that realization. The next day, when I complained to my neighbor about the previous night, he was very apologetic. Spirit offered me yet another lesson – practice forgiveness.

Each moment in life offers incredible opportunities if only we stay awake. To help us pay attention to each sacred moment and remain awake, I offer a simple process – *Observe, Accept, Forgive, Ask, Listen* and *Receive*. This practice dials down our mental propellers from fast to medium to slow. As our mind reduces its frantic whirling, a dimmer switch increases the light of consciousness.

Another flower with six petals demonstrates the circular process that takes us inward toward Home.

1. Observe.

We first observe, in a non-judgmental manner, our sensations, feelings, thoughts, relationships, communication and perceptions. This shifts our awareness to a different vantage point. We begin to notice where we're placing our attention. Are we shut down or connected with our senses? Are we fearful or calm? Are our thoughts replaying the past, focused on the present or anticipating the future? Are we defensive or relating to others from an open heart? Are we inhibited about expressing ourselves or honestly sharing? Are we side-tracked by others or are we living a life of purpose?

As we observe, we move our awareness inward. We may notice that our shoulders are tense, that we feel lonely, that we're preoccupied with work or that an internal critic is pushing us to achieve. We may also notice a hummingbird, fragrant roses or pictures of children. Whatever we observe is important, for it helps us pay attention to what's going on within and around us. That includes our needs, desires, actions, patterns and outcomes.

In the incident with my neighbor, I recognized my recurrent pattern of becoming overly busy and spending less time nurturing my body and relationships. Awakened, I saw the truth of the situation and that which laid beneath the surface, namely, embedded feelings of neglect. Insight led me to create balance and practice self-care.

Observation may call our attention to resonance or dissonance. These two forces act like an internal gyroscope. Resonance is a sympathetic vibration that causes contentment, peace and harmony, much like listening to a melodious sound. A string on a guitar resonates with another string plucked in the same note. Feeling goose bumps during a poignant moment offers another example of resonance.

Its opposite is dissonance, which is equally important in providing internal feedback. It signals disharmony and creates discomfort, fear, irritation and avoidance. If resonance is the magnetic force that draws us forward, dissonance is the force that pushes us backwards.

These two principles act in unison like a twin set of muscles. One expands while its opposite contracts. Both are valuable tools in observation. They tell us whether we resonate with activities, situations or people or, at the opposite extreme, whether we're repulsed by them. Resonance and dissonance teach us that certain sensations attract, others disgust; some thoughts generate love, others fear; certain sounds create harmony, others disharmony; some relationships produce an open heart, others constrict the heart; some visions trigger joy, others dread.

If I have an itch on my back and ask someone to relieve it, I would direct that person through a series of "yes's" and "no's" to reach the desired spot. The interplay of resonance and dissonance teaches me to be aware of my internal responses and guides me to that exact 'ah-h-h' moment.

The overall goal during observation is to maintain a neutral frame of mind while we pay attention to our lives. This helps us stay awake and focus on the now.

2. Accept

The next step is to accept ourselves exactly the way we are, with positive regard. This offsets the initial tendency to judge. This doesn't mean we have to agree with our thoughts, feelings or sensations, it merely suggests that we accept, in a loving manner, that we're thinking, feeling or sensing a certain way. Acceptance establishes a connection between us as observers and that which we're observing, an important step before any self-correction. Acceptance brings a sense of relief, for it cuts through denial. It acknowledges that we have courageously revealed our current state of being. It gently and lovingly moves us to a deeper awareness of our internal world.

For example, if I observe myself stuffing my body with food, I can move into judgment or acceptance. Rather than berating myself, I can accept the fact that I'm eating too much, too fast. I can also accept that my craving food is a form of self-soothing. This awareness shines light on my needs. I can then acknowledge that I have unmet needs that want to be satisfied.

3. Forgive

After we observe and accept, we move to forgive. Our critical minds can often kick us mercilessly for not acting, feeling or thinking as we should. Forgiveness offers a counter-measure to correct the mind and release judgments, preconceptions, resentments and guilt. It is the practice of letting go.

Forgiveness is not about condoning other people's behaviors. Rather, it is emptying the mind of discordant thoughts that act like poison. Holding onto poison doesn't punish others; it merely kills us. Through acts of forgiveness, we scrub our windows clean and allow the rays of compassion and peace to stream into our lives.

Forgiveness is one of the more difficult practices. The ego likes to be right. If we self-righteously point out that someone is wrong, we inflate the ego. We then join a mentality that prefers black and white, right versus wrong, winners over losers. However, whatever we do to others, we do to ourselves. Our projections emanate from the screen of our mind.

Forgiveness changes the movie that we are playing so we can perceive the world differently. So when we're being critical of ourselves, rather than beating up our minds with a statement such as, "You stupid moron, you made another mistake," we can say, "I forgive myself for making a mistake." It's obvious which statement brings peace.

4. Ask

Forgiveness, like the practice of observation or acceptance, may create a shift in consciousness. We move the process deeper when we ask for help from the Guiding Power of Spirit. Of course, we can ask for help anytime, but we tend to do so when we're in pain or in need. Actually, we can ask for help whenever we wish to stay connected with Spirit. We merely have to say, "Help me be still and return Home."

The very act of asking places the key of intention into the door of the Divine. Be assured that the door will open to guidance and love, not attack. Asking increases our faith in a higher power. The more we ask, the stronger our connection.

At the beginning of this chapter I described the episode in Sydney. When I traveled on the train, I asked for help when I was told to speak with the man sitting next to me. Asking created an immediate response.

5. Listen.

Once we ask we then must listen for the response. Listening is not easy in a fast-paced culture that bombards our senses. Listening requires that we reduce our internal chatter and expectations.

If we programmed a global positioning system in a car, we would have to listen for instructions. If the volume was low or we were chatting on a cell phone or with a passenger, we'd miss the instructions. The same would apply with our internal GPS.

To really listen, we have to quiet the mind and remain open to all possibilities. The messages may be different from the ones we expect or desire. If we are looking for the "right" answer, we may miss the message that is for our highest good. After all, our GPS has the best course figured out.

6. Receive

When we truly listen, we receive guidance. We may be lovingly instructed to do nothing or to take action. We may be advised to focus the mind, take better care of our bodies, forgive someone, or phone a friend. We may find some answers not to our liking because it disturbs the ego or interrupts our plans. And if we choose not to follow the guidance, Spirit doesn't counter-attack. It acts similar to a car's navigational system that calmly informs us that we've gone off course. Spirit continues to guide us in a loving manner. Whether we accept the advice is up to our own free will.

I have found that when I take direction from the Guiding Power of Spirit, my life flows. When I don't pay attention or resist the help, my life becomes a struggle. My GPS continually reminds me to slow down, take loving care of myself, create better balance in my life, and deepen my trust in Spirit.

The question often arises, "How do you distinguish the voice of ego from the voice of Spirit?" Ego operates from scarcity and speaks out of fear. Its messages are frantic, desperate, critical, controlling, seductive and manipulative. In contrast, the Guiding Power of Spirit beckons us with love and encouragement. It constantly and calmly conveys messages with an accepting, supportive and loving voice. It does take practice to distinguish between the voice of ego and Spirit. We'll explore this more extensively in a later chapter.

As our receptivity to Spirit increases, signposts appear more readily. A friend may call and offer advice; an article may appear on the Internet that answers a need. Symbols and synchronicity resonate with greater frequency. These signs strengthen belief in our GPS and reassure us we are going in the right direction.

The inward process of observing and accepting, forgiving and asking, listening and receiving creates a sacred space, an opening for Divine communion. The Buddha said that one can catch a glimpse of one's True Self in the space between thoughts. To do so, we must stay awake and be mindful of each moment.

We may have an easier time practicing being present in an environment surrounded by nature. Away from cell phones, computers and other distractions, we can expand awareness of our senses and become mindful of All That Is. We often forget to notice flowering plants or the phases of the moon. When we awaken to the natural world, we connect with all of life.

The next time you're outdoors, try this experiment. Find a space where you can be alone. It may be under a tree, near a body of water, or in a garden. After you center yourself, use your senses to observe your surroundings. Accept whatever you see, hear, touch, smell or taste. Then close your eyes and let go of your perceptions as if you have deleted the pictures in a digital camera. When you open your eyes, observe your environment through a new lens. You may notice a distant landscape or you may inspect the immediate area around you. Each time you close and open your eyes, find a fresh perspective. You may notice birds, clouds, insects or children.

Next, bring this expanded awareness to your inner world. Shut your eyes and ask for guidance such as, "Show me what I'm meant to do." If you listen for a loving message, you'll receive one. You may get an impulse to stand and stretch or you may be compelled to take a walk. You may feel the urge to remain still or you may hear words to a poem. As you practice without judgment in a natural setting away from busy distractions, you can be more observing, accept whatever is, forgive and let go, make a request, listen for a message, and receive an answer. This process connects you with your internal navigational system. It also forces you to face your resistance.

This occurred in the movie *Star Wars,* when Obi Wan Kenobi instructed Luke to feel the Force. Luke initially resisted guidance but eventually let go of his preconceptions. Like Luke, we are all in training to be Jedi Knights, awakening our internal guidance so we can feel the Force.

When we make a commitment to feel the Force, we set the intention to climb the transformational mountain. If we turn onto an errant path, our GPS will recalibrate without berating and guide us back on the road to inner peace.

Though we may try, we cannot force the Guiding Power of Spirit to point us in the direction of ego and separateness. That is akin to instructing a car's navigational system to go south when our destination is true north. Our GPS keeps us on track as long as we don't turn off the receiver. And when we encounter a problem, we ask for help. This doesn't mean we become robots and lose our free will. We merely walk freely with open eyes, rather than stumble in ignorance with eyes shut.

Staying awake and keeping our eyes open is like practicing yoga. We have to continually stretch our awareness beyond our egos so we can truly see. Our fellow travelers will often remind us to pay attention.

My dear friend, Bill Motlong, has known me for well over 35 years. We once worked together in a counseling center outside Chicago and much later participated in a men's support group. I call Bill my DNA brother. Though I now live in California and he and his wife, Barb, live in Wisconsin, we seem to encounter life lessons concurrently. Whether I'm talking about my worries, my need to be acknowledged, my wounds of neglect, my quest for Home, or my awe of the sacred, I know Bill will understand, for my issues are his issues and vice versa. During our phone conversations, we convey an open acceptance of each other's process and freely challenge any misperceptions. We inevitably end our conversations with greater clarity of our lessons and a deeper appreciation of Spirit who has joined us as soul brothers to keep each other awake. We also laugh heartily at our egos' futile attempts to retain complete control.

In addition to friends or family, strangers can also play a part in our awakening process. I once attended a personal growth seminar and was asked to pair off with another participant. I hoped to avoid the woman, since she smelled like a chain-smoker. She was dressed shabbily and seemed rather cantankerous. During the exercise we were asked to look at each other and connect with our eyes. I felt revolted by the smell of tobacco, but as soon as I peered into her eyes I was awestruck. There was an instant bond, as if our eyes peered into each other's soul. My preconceptions, like a cloud of smoke, dissolved. I experienced an amazing awakening. She was no longer separate but a kindred spirit. We gave each other a loving smile and a hug.

Everyone we meet can assist us if we remember to stay awake. They may keep us from wandering aimlessly and remind us of our ultimate destination. Our commitment to stay awake and the Guiding Power of Spirit help us move to the next challenging stage – **Healing Wounds and Breaking Free**.

MAPPING EXERCISE

This exercise will take you through the process of Observing, Accepting, Forgiving, Asking, Listening and Receiving. Have your journal ready.

Think of a disturbing incident that affects you personally. It may relate to a family member, health concern, finances, partner, career or other personal issue. As you imagine the incident, let your stream of consciousness highlight any thoughts that disturb you. Notice any resonance and dissonance.

Observe this without judgment. Then write about the event in your journal. Include any unresolved feelings. Notice any resistance or inhibition about externalizing your thoughts on paper. After you have completed writing, put your journal down. Read what you have recorded.

Accept whatever is there, for there is no right or wrong. Acknowledge that you have courageously revealed yourself. That deserves recognition and love. Notice any shifts in consciousness.

Forgive yourself for having any disturbing thoughts or feelings. You may want to release fear, anger, resentment or sadness. Practice forgiveness by completing the phrase, "I forgive myself for . . ." You could also use the words, "I release . . ." or, "I let go of . . ." Complete the phrase with whatever you wish to release; i.e., "I let go of my resentment and anger," or, "I forgive myself for being critical." Write the sentences in your journal and then repeat them out loud. Notice your response. Emotions may appear. Release them. Allow yourself to stay awake.

Ask the Guiding Power of Spirit to assist you. You could ask, "Help me find inner peace." You could add a specific request like, "Help me heal," or, "Help me release anger and fear."

Listen for a response. Sit in silence. Become aware of your breathing. Let your breathing take you deeper within. Notice any shifts in your senses, mood or thoughts. Listen and be open.

Receive. Allow whatever comes to come. If you feel inclined to write the messages in your journal, do so. Let the words flow on the page. If writing is distracting, concentrate on receiving. Notice what you experience. Guidance may come as a gentle voice, an intuitive sense, an image, or physical sensation. Notice the messages that resonate. You are learning to stay awake.

GUIDED VISUALIZATION

Return to a relaxing place, free of distractions. Set the mood. Become mindful of the inhalation and exhalation of your breaths. Notice the pause between breaths. Let each breath expand your awareness.

Now imagine walking through a fog. It prevents you from seeing. You know you're headed toward the seashore because you hear a distant foghorn and catch a glimpse of light emanating from a lighthouse. You feel separate and alone, unsure of your location. The only sure thing is the deep longing inside, a longing to see.

Your bare feet touch the sand and you walk several paces. You find a resting place and sit down. You close your eyes and allow your mind to be still. You become aware of your body and feel your flesh, your cravings and longings. You notice the senses that connect you with the outside world. You smell the ocean and taste a hint of salt in the air. You hear the waves slapping against the shore. You feel a cool breeze against your cheeks. The coolness is soon replaced by warmth. The rays of the sun bathe your face and brighten your life. The earth absorbs tension from your body and a fresh wind clears stagnant energy. The sound of the ocean purifies your thoughts. A loving energy enters your body and penetrates every cell. You open your eyes. The fog has disappeared.

You awaken to a tropical paradise. You marvel at the sparkling rays glittering like diamonds off the deep blue ocean. You inhale the scent of fragrant flowers. A gentle rhythm of waves mirrors the tempo of your breathing. You watch colorful, tropical birds flying overhead. With a blue sky and warm nurturing sun overhead, you stand up and stroll toward the water.

You become aware of your inner child who wants to play. You let the dear little one splash in the refreshing sea, playing with abandon, happy to be free. The child squeals with delight at a crashing wave and giggles at a surfacing pod of dolphins. They join the child and, together, they frolic in the surf. One dolphin guides the child onto its back and leaps across the water toward a distant island.

This is an island of awareness. Senses are magnified and illusions have disappeared. A double rainbow arcs across the blue sky. Near the beach your child jumps off the dolphin and rushes to the golden sand. The child is awake. And so are you.

You realize that everything that happens to you has a Divine purpose for your highest good. You know that you are loved and cared for just the way you are. Your heart opens; your chest expands. Love and acceptance flow through you.

The loving energy moves to your throat. You hum a joyful hymn of gratitude. Your third eye opens and you receive a vision of the interconnectedness with All That Is. You are awake. And so are your body, emotions, mind, heart, voice and vision. You resonate with peace and harmony.

On the beach you notice an ancient chest. It beckons you. Before you open the lid, you make a special request. This request may be for healing, for love, or for anything your heart desires. You ask and open the lid. You receive whatever is there.

Notice what you find. Notice also your response. Even if the chest is empty, you have received a gift. In time you will know its true meaning. Embrace this gift in this special place. Stay as long as you desire.

When you're ready to walk back into your current life, bring your beautiful gift, your joyful inner child, and your increased awareness into the present. You are ready to view the world with amazing grace. You once were lost but now are found. No longer blind, you now can see.

Take a few moments and record your thoughts or impressions in your journal.

CHAPTER SIX

HEALING WOUNDS AND BREAKING FREE

Conscious awareness, insight, and "working through" . . . is the best path

I know to the acceptance of our highest powers.

– Abraham Maslow

Mother's Day weekend. I visited my 96-year-old mother, who resides in a nursing home in Ohio near my sister and brother-in-law. Though she has dementia, my mother appears to watch the world through the sparkling eyes of an innocent child.

During my visit, I asked her if I was her brother, her son or her father. She thought a moment and then responded with utmost confidence, "You are all of them." She obviously knew more about Oneness of Spirit than I imagined.

When I asked her if she knew my name, she paused again and then answered, "Accept."

Dementia may have caused my mother to lose her rational faculties but it didn't mean she had lost contact with Spirit. I accepted the message.

I handed her a present and her face glowed as if it was the very first gift she ever received. In her mind it probably was. She struggled with the wrapping and I told her to pull the ribbon to release the bow.

She furrowed her brow and gave me a quizzical look as she asked, "Are you sure?"

Upon hearing her question, I immediately burst into laughter. My laughter prompted my mother to giggle and before long we were both unable to contain ourselves, each infecting the other to laugh like two little kids. God only knows what the staff thought about our shenanigans. When we eventually calmed down, I realized that the hilarious moment clearly demonstrated the power of healing.

As a child I often heard my mother ask the question, "Are you sure?" whenever I responded affirmatively to any of her requests. It didn't matter whether I *had* emptied the garbage or finished my homework. My mother double checked everything with, "Are you sure?" That was her way. Mind you, not the best way to build self-confidence in a child, for I learned to always question myself.

The same question in the nursing home triggered neither anxiety nor lack of confidence. Rather it provoked laughter – lots of laughter. And it seemed as if both my mother and I were in on the joke. The fact that I saw humor in the situation represented a significant healing shift that had long since taken place.

The healing power of laughter proved that the scared little boy who grew up insecure and unsure had come a long way toward releasing those toxic beliefs. Of that I was sure.

Healing brings the light of Spirit into the dark recesses of our mind so we can clear unwelcome beliefs that prevent us from coming Home. Healing raises our consciousness and shifts our perspective. This alters the narrative and outcome to our story. As we change our interaction with the world, anxiety, sadness or anger can transform into loving acceptance and humor.

Conscious awareness of our wounds helps us break free from the limitations they impose. Wounding taught us about fear and pain and resulted in beliefs about not existing or feeling, not thinking or being loved, not speaking or being heard, not being seen or being connected with All That Is.

The Guiding Power of Spirit helps us overcome those obstacles that prevent us from reaching the pinnacle. Acceptance and love provide soothing balm as we face roadblocks, tunnels, narrow passages and detours on the mountain toward realization. The climb requires perseverance, faith and courage. However, the knowledge that we are seeking a higher path keeps us moving upward.

Healing can sometimes be a tortuous journey that requires great dedication. It demands a willingness to be awakened from a numbed existence and reclaim our little orphans. It asks that we break through denial, grieve lost parts of ourselves, and let go. Healing may require that we share our story with others and dissolve the toxins and pointed barbs that told us we weren't worthy to be protected, loved and cared for. We may also witness other people's stories and honor their healing, for as we help them we assist our own healing.

Surprisingly, my time with my mother afforded both of us quiet time. Though she may not have understood what I was saying, I felt free to talk about my childhood. My mother was always so busy tending to the practicalities of raising four children and holding down a factory job that I rarely talked to her about my feelings. Yet during my visit over Mother's Day, we had time to share. It wasn't too late to relate my stories and my feelings. As I held my mother's arthritic hands, I laughed at some of my childhood capers. She giggled in response. I told her of my deep appreciation for her many years of sacrifice that allowed her children to achieve in life. I cried tears of gratitude for that special moment with my mother. Though she had dementia, my mother was there for me. I realized that in her own way, she was always there for me when I was a child. I told her how much I loved her. She squeezed my hands and said, "You're great." I hugged her and felt the healing resonate through our souls.

In strange and wonderful ways, the Guiding Power of Spirit illuminates areas that need healing and correction. The dark tunnel of fear may prevent us from seeing the light, but as we honestly face any festering wounds, we heal them. The torch of love releases the mental anguish stamped in our psyche that constantly remind us of wounding experiences.

I once gashed my elbow in a bicycle accident. At the emergency room, the doctor scrubbed and flushed the wound thoroughly before applying sutures. If he hadn't spent time removing the dirt and grit, the wound would have become infected. Most of us have wounds that have never been cleaned out. They may be wounds of neglect, abandonment, lack of acceptance or love, or even of narcissistic entitlement that leads to self-absorption.

We all have emotional grit that has been suppressed and forgotten. Wounds still impact our lives if they remain emotionally charged. Abuse and neglect often get replayed even when we are adults. Healing, therefore, requires that we uncover the source of wounding, clean out the debris, add corrective balm, and foster a healing environment.

Healing wounds and breaking free is a step-by-step process of restoration. In the previous chapter, I discussed building a foundation of observing, accepting, forgiving, asking, listening and receiving guidance. Those principles will shed light on any blockages in the body, emotions, mind, relationships, communication and perception.

Before we can install new software, we must run a virus scan to identify and remove the corrupted files. I call my anti-virus program **IRSPEA**, an acronym for: *Inspect, Reject, Select, Project, Expect* and *Accept.*

Another six-petaled flower represents the anti-virus program. Let's review each concept.

Inspect Your Life

The truth is that our finest moments are most likely to occur when we are feeling deeply uncomfortable, unhappy, or unfulfilled. For it is only in such moments . . . that we are likely to step out of our ruts and start searching for different ways or truer answers. – M. Scott Peck

When we observe, we watch dispassionately: when we inspect, we examine purposefully. Inspection is similar to the Fourth Step in the Twelve Step Traditions, where we are asked to take a fearless moral inventory. An accepting, nonjudgmental attitude helps us examine beliefs that create homelessness. Identifying the corrosive messages undermines their authority and is the first step toward corrective action.

You can approach your life like an artist scanning a painting. The canvas represents your life colored by your thoughts and beliefs. You can produce a three-dimensional picture when you inspect your painting from the following perspectives.

1. The whole picture. On first glance you might view the picture as a whole with its many shades of colors and form a general impression. What is the mood of the painting? What aspects of your life please you? What areas need touch-ups or reconstruction?

2. The edges. Upon closer examination, you might notice the specific beliefs that play out in your life. Can you identify the thoughts that make you edgy or contribute to low self-esteem or feelings of unworthiness? What beliefs nourish self-care?

3. Patterns. You might then detect some recurring patterns, such as withdrawing from intimacy or engaging in conflict, working long hours or taking care of others. Can you recognize your positive and negative patterns?

4. Foreground/background. You might notice the foreground, that which catches your immediate attention like health, finances or relationships. In the background, your embedded beliefs continually paint a programmed picture on your life's canvas. What issues are currently occupying your attention? What are the underlying beliefs?

5. Empty spaces. If you scanned the painting, you might eventually see the empty spaces, or that which is missing in your life. What are the needs, wants and desires that are not being satisfied?

When I lived in Chicago, I conducted hypnosis seminars at a cancer support center. Those who attended were in various stages of cancer. Pain was real yet the courageous souls moved deeper inside and inspected their beliefs as they sought to live with a life-threatening illness. Many discovered the viral programs running in the background, altered their beliefs, and renovated their bodies. In the process, they prioritized what was important and meaning-ful. Some bodies healed completely; others passed away. As they reconnected with the Guiding Power of Spirit, they taught me, "You can come back to life even when you're dying." In order to come back to life, we must be relentless in our review.

Though I am upbeat, energetic and adventurous on the whole, I continually discover mental programs that trigger wounds of ne-glect, fear, guilt and shame. My childhood was etched in hardship and taught me that life was a struggle. However, it also taught me to be resourceful, resilient and self-sufficient. Humor offered a release for tension.

I heard few positive affirmations as a child and rarely, if ever, heard the words, "I love you." As a result, I didn't talk about my accomplishments. I learned that self-praise was no recommenda-tion. I didn't realize the extent of this virus until after my own children were born. They grew up with two loving parents who offered a regular diet of praising affirmations. Strangely, my chil-dren's abundance made me face my own malnourished parts.

Looking at my life's picture, I can see many patterns. My hunger for love and acknowledgment has often led me to over-accommodate and seek perfection. In the process, I can neglect myself and feel overwhelmed. This prompts self criticism and projection of my inadequacy onto others. This viral program was passed down from my parents who, no doubt, picked it up from previous generations.

To avoid pain, I move into a pattern of getting busy – a family trait. When life gets too easy and comfortable, I create other proj-ects that can become overwhelming and flip me back to struggle. I then neglect my orphaned self, little Lenny, who wants to have fun and play. Finding balance is an ongoing challenge.

The foreground of my life is a fervent commitment to live my truth and remain connected to Spirit. However, my ego often plays havoc in the background, stirring up fear. Anxiety and worry about being victimized can catapult me back to a past that needs further healing.

Since I tend to be self-reliant and independent, I often create empty spaces lacking support. That touches many aspects of my life including business, play and relationships. Interestingly, my writing is a solitary endeavor that reinforces this. Yet, it also serves as a healing medium when I create enough space to "do nothing" – guilt-free activity to play (write) with abandon.

As I review my life, I highlight those files that create disharmony and homelessness. Mine are about survival, neglect, struggle, invisibility, inhibition, aloneness, separateness, unworthiness, financial insecurity, scarcity and fear. At the same time, I acknowledge those beliefs I wish to expand – inner power, creativity, ease, expression, recognition, partnership, connection, bounty, harmony and love.

The process of inspection is a time of reflection. However, we may not be able to see our own blind spots. Therefore, we'll need mirrors to inspect those hard-to-get-at places. Relationships, mentors, coaches, therapists, spiritual advisers, colleagues and friends can show us what we can't see.

My first experience with such mirrors occurred in college. I attended seminary at a time when the encounter movement was popular. Each dorm would gather together to encounter one another during a series of evenings when we evaluated each other. At the sessions, we offered frank feedback to one another about how we came across as well as our strengths and weaknesses. Most of us expected the worse. Surprisingly, we were offered wonderful feedback and incredible gifts of insight into our personalities. To this day, I still remember many of the comments.

Once we have a clear picture of our life, we can rewrite the script and alter our story. But first, we must purge the corrupted files.

Reject and Release That Which You No Longer Want

I am an old man who has had many worries, most of which have never happened to me. – Mark Twain

During the editing phase of a novel, an author has numerous choices. S/he can eliminate dialogue, themes, characters and scenes, or add new ones. Here, we are about to delete those toxic elements that negatively impact our stories. These are viruses, or corrosive beliefs, that we thought were true.

Releasing doesn't mean we spend all our time rejecting thoughts. It means we make a conscious decision to eliminate debilitating images that appear during the thousands of conversations we have in our mind. Embedded in our daily "self-talk" are countless beliefs that tell us how to look after ourselves, how to think and feel, how to relate and communicate, and how to see the world. Unless we scrub the viruses that infect our lives, we'll always have them with us, running in the background.

Rejecting is a nothing more than highlighting those unwelcome words, phrases and paragraphs in our stories and deleting them. Choosing and editing are necessary aspects of life. They sharpen and clarify our message. When an emotional passage of a story no longer serves us, it's time to let go. Forgiveness releases the emotional attachment to a viral belief so we can move on to the next chapter. Otherwise, we'll be caught in a circular loop of reliving past stories.

This can be particularly difficult because the ego resists efforts that threaten its control. It has an investment in maintaining the status quo even when the files are corrupted. Therefore, if we want to uninstall a victimhood program, we have to bypass the ego and reconfigure the computer.

Rejecting that which we no longer want leads to freedom. When we reject silence, denial, suppression, dishonesty, neglect, shame, guilt, fear or a closed heart, we open ourselves to their opposite.

I suggest that you identify the noxious themes that play havoc in your life. You could have beliefs about the body (I'm fat and ugly); about self-worth (I'm not good enough); about will power (I can't complete anything); about relationships (I can't trust anyone to love me); about communication (I can't express myself); or about vision (If I dream big, I'll only get disappointed). You can have corrosive beliefs about money (I never have enough); about jobs (No one appreciates what I do); and about other significant aspects of your life such as health, success and God.

Since much of our wounding occurred during childhood, that's the place to look for the viral programs that belong in the trash can. They created our little orphans and took us away from our True Self. The mapping exercise at the end of this chapter will help you take inventory of some of these toxic beliefs. Here are some examples of the beliefs I downloaded from my parents.

- *Life is a struggle.*
- *Don't just sit there, do something; get busy.*
- *I can't have fun when there's work to be done.*
- *Self-praise is no recommendation.*
- *I'm not loveable, worthy or good enough.*
- *I'm not capable.*
- *Sadness is a sign of weakness. Don't be vulnerable.*
- *I must be in control to protect and care for myself.*
- *I must be perfect to achieve approval and success.*
- *My needs will not be met in a relationship.*
- *Relationships are fraught with conflict and struggle.*
- *Love doesn't last.*
- *I can't rely on others.*
- *Men are to be feared.*
- *Women are really in control.*
- *Sex and guilt go hand in hand.*
- *If I'm visible, I will be attacked.*
- *There's never enough.*
- *Money's the root of all evil.*
- *I don't deserve abundance.*

After we've identified the negative beliefs, we can delete them by letting go. This takes us back to forgiveness. It may seem odd to practice forgiveness for having a virus in our memory banks, but forgiveness severs the emotional investment. For example, if I don't forgive myself for believing life is a struggle, I'll feel guilty for having the belief in the first place.

We can eject the downloaded files by saying, "I forgive myself for believing . . . and I now let go of that belief." When we release the virus, we step into the next petal.

Select Affirming Thoughts and Beliefs

It's not enough to have a good mind. The main thing is to use it well. – Descartes

Now that we've rejected self-defeating thoughts, the next step is to select those healing nuggets of gold. These are affirming statements and declarations that we now want to hold dear to our heart. They are the words our little orphan always wanted to hear. They will relate, in some way or another, to healing our body, emotions, mind, heart, voice and vision.

We act like authors when we select words that have intention. They shape our narratives and stories. Therefore, it's important to select words and phrases that counter any wounding virus. We want to create a vibrant picture of love, healing and connection to Spirit. The phrases we select then become our new internal dialogue or self-talk.

When connected with our GPS, we receive downloads of life-changing wisdom. We may be directed to improve our health, shift our feelings, focus the mind, expand the heart, express our voice, or identify a mission. The signposts that we have observed along the way will point us toward that which needs healing. When we selectively reinforce new messages, we embed them in our psyche.

Since I enjoy a good laugh, I wouldn't necessarily select an affirmation about having a sense of humor. Instead, I would choose a toxic belief that needs healing such as, "I'm not loveable, worthy or good enough," and replace it with an affirming message, "I am loved and cherished." It's important to frame any healing nugget with a positive emotional statement in the first person and in the present tense. Since our mind takes our words literally, it's best to avoid negatives (I won't) or future references (I will).

Positive declarations can convey healing about the body (I am healthy and take loving care of my body); about self-worth (I deserve love and success); about empowerment (I am powerful and decisive); about relationships (I open my heart to love); about communication (I honestly and openly express myself); or about vision (I am exceptionally successful). You can create new beliefs about money (I am abundant and prosperous); about jobs (I have a wonderful career that recognizes my talents and rewards me financially) or any other aspect of your life.

Here's a list of some of my healing declarations:

- *My life is easy and effortless.*
- *I am safe and secure, loved and protected.*
- *I am healthy and energetic and create a balanced life.*
- *I love and accept myself exactly as I am.*
- *I joyously create time to have fun and experience pleasure.*
- *I am exceptional and unique.*
- *I deserve financial success, which comes easily and effortlessly.*
- *Personal power and I are one.*
- *I confidently achieve my goals.*
- *I enjoy my success.*
- *I have all that I need.*
- *Every dollar I circulate returns to me with compounded interest.*
- *I express my truth and live a life of purpose.*
- *I heal others with my words.*
- *I am recognized for who I am.*
- *I balance my masculine and feminine sides.*
- *I welcome a loving community into my life.*
- *I still my mind and listen to Spirit.*
- *My body, feelings, mind, heart, voice and vision serve Spirit.*
- *I trust in the Divine and embrace inner peace.*

Often, fear and limitation can immobilize us from selecting beliefs that take us off the valley floor. If we choose small, we climb a molehill. If we select grand, we scale Mount Everest. Ego may try and hold us back, but Spirit always encourages us forward.

If we remain hesitant about reaching high, we can talk with a friend, therapist or life coach. An outsider can offer another perspective and, more likely than not, will recognize our potential for prosperity, health, love and spiritual fulfillment.

Once we select new files and programs, we're ready for installation.

Project New Thoughts and Images

Thought coupled with action creates your destiny. – Stuart Wilde

With a script in hand for our new story, we have a number of powerful tools at our disposal to project the ideas inward and outward as we climb the transformative mountain. Let's take a closer look at some projective devices: Directed Meditation; Active Imagination; Declarations; Congruent Action; and Emotionally Corrective Experiences.

Directed Meditation. Since the mind operates like a transmitter, both sending and receiving information, we want to generate more power before projecting messages. Meditation, as a method to still the mind, helps us move away from our internal chatter toward that empty place between thoughts. Counting breaths, repeating a mantra, focusing on a spiritual figure, connecting with love, and practicing mindfulness are some of the popular methods of meditation. Numerous studies have demonstrated the benefits of meditation in reducing stress, promoting healing, improving concentration, and increasing health and wellbeing.

While the primary goal of meditation is to quiet the mind and remain in the present, the purpose of *directed* meditation is to achieve the same results so we can install a new program. It is similar to self-hypnosis in that it slows the whirling mental propellers and permits us to transmit clearly without static. If the wind machine in the mind howls with a gale force, our precious messages will be scattered. Therefore, we must create a fertile field to seed our new beliefs.

The process we learned in the previous chapter about observing, accepting, forgiving, asking, listening and receiving taught us about consciously shifting our mental state to be receptive to internal guidance. We now want to expand that receptivity and direct the mind. Directed meditation is nothing more than entering a state where we bypass the critical, judgmental mind and implant suggestions.

Whenever we watch a movie, we enter an altered state because we, in effect, suspend our disbelief to enjoy the film. Otherwise our critical mind would continually harass us, "This is not real." Since we now want to project a new film on the internal screen, we must suspend disbelief. To do that we must create a place free of distractions – a mental movie theater where we can dim the lights before the projector starts showing new affirming images.

You may have seen movies that were introduced with a countdown of numbers from ten to one. In the same way, directed meditation counts the mind downward from a busy ten to a serene and tranquil one to produce an alpha state. You can imagine a spiral staircase with ten stairs leading you deeper within your mind. Each descending stair takes you downward, deeper, to the bottom of the staircase where you find yourself relaxed and receptive.

The guided visualizations at the end of each chapter are meant to create such an experience. You can choose one of them to practice moving inward. It will, however, take some training. You don't become a black-belt meditator overnight. The instructor of my first meditation class some 30 years ago informed the students that if we meditated every day for three months, we would change our lives. His emphatic statement proved true. Over time, meditation alters the way we relate to the world as we begin to quiet the monkey mind, chattering away. It takes ongoing practice and discipline, like regular exercise.

You can expand your meditation practice by taking classes on meditation or self-hypnosis, or meditating with a group or listening to visualizations. They'll help you deepen the relaxation response. When you have learned how to dim the house lights, you are more open to suggestion. You can then project your new picture with power and clarity.

Active Imagination. You are comfortably settled at the theater and turn on the projector. You now employ active imagination to conjure images, thoughts and feelings. This allows you to actively create on the wide screen of your mind with the surround-sound of your five senses. You paint multi-textured images and interact with them as you want your story to unfold.

Elite athletes visualize peak performances to enhance their game. Phil Jackson, who successfully coached the Chicago Bulls to six championships and then the Los Angeles Lakers to four championships, described his use of meditation and visualization in *Sacred Hoops*. He wrote, "Visualization is the bridge I use to link the grand vision of the team I conjure up every summer to the evolving reality on the court. That vision becomes a working sketch that I adjust, refine and sometimes scrap altogether as the season develops."[1]

Phil said that he visualized 45 minutes before each game as a method of preparing his mind. His use of active imagination painted a picture of positive outcomes for his basketball team. He promoted these concepts among his players, and the fact that he's won more championships than any other coach in the NBA is a true testament to his coaching and his techniques.

You can utilize the same principle of Active Imagination and program your mind with powerful mental pictures that replicate any desired state. If you actively imagine yourself as a loving and abundant human being, you, in effect, download those images onto your mental screensaver.

You can also use active imagination for health, success, problem solving and relationships. When your little orphan needs comfort and healing, you can imagine your adult self surrounding the orphan with love. A powerful imagination can replace any disturbing picture with a beautiful visual image. As you project, so shall you receive.

Declarations. Most movies use dialogue to reinforce themes. Likewise, the words we use create our narrative. When we make a declaration, we set in motion the law of cause and effect. A declaration is a verbal reminder of our new affirmations. Initially, we may feel uneasy about our positive phrases but, over time, we grow into them. They become us. But we have to constantly hear the words to believe them. They reverse those noxious messages we were told while growing up.

When I attended the Family Institute Program in Chicago back in 1974, I participated in a psychodrama where participants re-enacted each other's family scenarios to highlight the dramas in order to create new outcomes. At one point, the facilitator instructed me to tell the couple role-playing my parents, "I love you and I love myself." I choked on words that were never uttered in my household. It became clear back then that my healing was about learning to express love to myself and to others. Those nurturing words have since become my beloved friends.

Stating a declaration once is not enough. It must be memorized and repeated, especially when we're feeling the opposite. Since we heard childhood beliefs thousands of times, we can counteract those thoughts by frequently surrounding ourselves with affirming messages. This anchors them to our unconscious.

The old saying, "Out of sight, out of mind," holds true. You want to create the opposite condition, placing your declarations in sight so you can hold them in your mind. I suggest writing the declarations down and placing them near an area where you spend time such, as your computer, office or car. Read them twice daily, soon after you wake up and before you retire for the night. Those two fertile periods offer a wonderful opportunity to seed your mind.

A vision board is another way to display declarations in picture format. You can create a cut-and-paste collage or a computerized version. If you choose cut-and-paste, scan through magazines to find images and words that highlight the declarations, intentions and end results of what you want to create and experience. Glue the pictures on a poster board and place it where it can be easily seen. One of mine hangs in the bedroom and the other is framed in my office. I also took a snapshot of one for the screensaver on my cell phone. The word, "Wow" pops out at me whenever I make a call.

If you create a computer version, you have access to all kinds of pictures. You can include photos of your family or role models and craft diagrams of your purpose-filled life. The computer-generated model of the vision board is probably faster than the cut-and-paste approach, but some of us like to play with scissors and glue. Discover what works for you.

Vision boards can be general or very specific. On one of my boards, I had pasted a picture of a blue Toyota to replace my old car. When I packed my belongings for the move from Chicago, I stored the vision board in a carton. After I moved, many of my boxes still hadn't been opened and I was so busy setting up my new home that I had neglected to unpack the vision board. Since I sold my car in Chicago, I needed a new one. I had forgotten about the image of the car but my psyche did not. The first dealer offered me a gold car off the lot with a good price. The second dealer offered a better price and told me, "I have a car available with all your specifications. It's a beautiful blue." It was the exact same color as my vision board. Needless to say, it's the car I drive.

A vision board will not only help you stay focused but also accountable. You increase the magnitude of thought when you announce to the world, "This is who I am." Seeing your vision everyday lets you know where you're heading and what you need to accomplish. I also suggest telling your supportive friends about your declarations. By doing so, you enlist others to help you stay focused. You also become more invested and committed because your word is on the line.

Many years ago I made a public declaration to my men's group that I was a professional writer. That very act reinforced my personal commitment to write as a consummate professional and spurred me forward in my writing career.

As you work with declarations, I suggest you periodically upgrade them with more powerful and expansive ones. This takes your narrative to greater heights.

Congruent Action. Our behaviors, thoughts and feelings echo each other. Therefore, as we adopt new beliefs, it is imperative that we act in a congruent fashion to meld them together.

If I talk on the phone while reclining comfortably in a chair, I'm more apt to relate in a relaxed manner. However, if I change my body posture and stand, I'll send a message to my brain that I'm ready to end the conversation. If I act depressed, more likely than not I will feel depressed and think depressed thoughts. If I act in a loving manner, I will generate loving emotions and thoughts.

When we change the way we behave, we alter the way we think and feel. And when we change our thoughts or shift emotions, we change our behaviors. Once we make a conscious decision to act congruently with our declarations and new mental pictures, we create a potent chain reaction.

For example, if I declare, "I am courageous," I must commit random acts of courage to reinforce the corresponding belief and feeling. When I act courageous and rebuff fear, I feel more courageous and strengthen my declaration and image of myself as a man of courage. Congruent action, when practiced repeatedly, integrates behavior with belief and emotions and, over time, becomes a habit.

To avoid overload, it's better to work with one belief at a time. For some, it may involve the practice of self-love, for others it may take the form of embracing abundance. As we climb our mountain and walk with greater confidence, we can scale more difficult terrain.

No doubt, there will be times when acting out the declaration seems totally foreign. In those instances, you may have to pretend or act "as if" you believed. When actors play a role, they think, feel and act like a character in order to portray themselves as believable. In order to feel the part, you sometimes have to act the part.

When I first began working on prosperity consciousness, I had difficulty conjuring the feeling of financial abundance. Having been raised in a cash-strapped household, I was taught that money comes from hard manual labor and that most rich people were crooks – not exactly wealth-conscious beliefs. After taking several seminars on wealth-building, I still couldn't feel what it was like to have lots of cash. Whenever I accumulated money, I spent it on education or travel, both worthy endeavors, but my savings account never grew.

So one morning I put on my only suit and went to the nearest bank. I asked to see the manager and told him I was anticipating a windfall of a large some of money, possibly a million dollars. I figured anything was possible with the mind. Not surprisingly, the manager ushered me into his office, offered me coffee and outlined options to get the maximum return. After being treated like a million dollars, I visited another bank nearby and re-enacted the same scenario. The response was similar. It felt wonderful being treated with such respect. And I came to believe it *was* actually possible to have more money. All this because I acted "as if" I was wealthy.

I have since learned that real wealth has nothing to do with money. It's more about acknowledging the abundance around us. That could be friendships, health and love. That perspective, of course, gets reinforced through congruent action.

Emotionally Corrective Experiences. Deep wounds require intense healing. An emotionally corrective experience provides a counterbalance to debilitating trauma. It's like replacing a knee with a bionic part. Intense positive exchanges flush toxins from wounds and enable us to walk tall.

Imagine a tearful young boy who arrives home from school, distraught about being bullied. He finds his father, who lovingly wraps his arms around him and consoles him. The loving display comforts his son and provides a potent message that he can return home for support and gather strength. There's nothing more powerful than the love of parents who build a child's self-worth and self-esteem.

If we did not have nurturing parents to provide such corrective experiences, we can assume responsibility to find our own healing opportunities. If we felt physically, emotionally or mentally shut down, unloved, inhibited or invisible, we can counteract those experiences. One of the natural arenas of healing occurs in loving friendships and partnerships. They provide opportunities to expand the heart and communicate loving thoughts and feelings.

Of course, relationships can be painful, but even with pain, healing occurs if we raise into consciousness the shadows of unresolved issues such as abandonment, abuse or neglect. When a partner or friend acts in our highest good, helps us see who we are, flaws and all, and loves us just the same, we receive a potent healing elixir.

Such corrective experiences may occur spontaneously or they may need to be sought out. Self-help groups, such as twelve-step programs, provide a welcoming environment of openness, honesty, fellowship and support to offset the dysfunctional childhood programming of denial and suppression. For others, personal growth workshops offer avenues to release emotions and implant healing messages. Some may prefer the confidential nature of therapy to engage in one-on-one work to deal with traumatic issues. Then again, others may seek spiritual practices and rituals that tap into the healing power of Spirit.

On my personal journey I've had numerous corrective emotional experiences. The first major one occurred in the Catholic seminary where I found a nurturing environment with an incredible group of young men. We were mentored by fathers who genuinely cared for their flock. Though I left after college, I know my character underwent a radical transformation as a result of the positive and, often healing, interactions with other men.

My other corrective emotional experiences have covered a variety of modalities including personal growth seminars, psychotherapy, men's groups, couple's therapy, sensitivity groups, breathwork, Neuro-Linguistic Programming, healing touch, chakra balancing, hypnosis, shamanic journeying, vision quests in nature, yoga weekends, and spiritual retreats. They all served to move me further up my personal mountain. Mind you, I had to dig my way through plenty of landslides.

There's an old saying that when the student is ready, a teacher will appear. The same applies to healing. When you're ready for healing, a healer will appear. All you need is the willingness to be healed. Spirit is always at your side and knows what you need and how to dig you out. Be patient. A bulldozer will materialize and help you clear the rubble.

Expect Positive Results

Sometimes success is due less to ability than to zeal. – Charles Buxton

Healing is more likely to occur *if* you expect it. And if you expect a negative outcome, that's probably what you'll get. This concept was labeled the Pygmalion Effect, and is often demonstrated in studies such as the one where a group of teachers were told some students were gifted, when in fact they were not. The teachers gave them special treatment and amazingly, the students improved their test performance. The reverse also occurred. Teachers who believed students were not bright, when in actual fact they had high IQ's, gave them less attention than other students, and the resulting test scores showed a decline.

Another example of the power of expectation is the placebo effect. Placebo is the Latin word for "I shall please." It draws upon a person's beliefs and the suggestibility about a treatment, such as taking a pill, to reduce symptoms. The placebo effect can result in improvement in up to 35 to 60 percent of those who participate, and with certain trials the percentage increases further. The placebo actually affects the body's biochemistry, including the immune system and hormones, and clearly demonstrates the power of belief.

The bottom line – expect a successful outcome when you climb your mountain. It may not unfold exactly as you anticipate but, with perseverance and repetition, expect to arrive at the top. Recognize the signposts along the way. They'll indicate you're on the right track.

It must be said, however, that as you install healing thoughts, you'll probably experience cognitive dissonance. This concept means that contradictory messages create dissonance. It occurs when a new thought conflicts with a previously embedded idea. It's as if your computer has two competing programs running at the same time. For example, you introduce an optimistic declaration, "I am exceptional and unique." The old program immediately counters with criticism, "If you believe THAT, it means you're REALLY stupid."

When the internal battle rages, the immediate inclination is to debate the corrosive belief, "No, I'm not stupid." This merely perpetuates the struggle. Avoid the conflict by recognizing that you are making progress. The fact that you're experiencing internal resistance means that your mental computer has recognized that you're replacing an old program. Downloading a new program may take time. Be patient. Honor the installation process. The outmoded beliefs have been with you for many years. They will want to hang around. Don't battle with the old; merely project the new.

Repetition and consistency are our allies. Successful athletes practice, practice and practice. In the process, they create muscle memories so they don't have to think, they merely react. We want to create a similar process. Repetition will embed our beliefs. After awhile, they'll run unconsciously in the background.

Supposedly, it takes 21 days for an egg to hatch. Imagine if you persistently focused on a declaration over the same period of time with great expectation. You repeated the words and visualized the images in the morning and at night and even threw in a few extra moments during the day. And if you experienced a discouraging relapse, you immediately recalled the words of e.e. cummings – "To be nobody-but-yourself – in a world which is doing its best, night and day, to make you somebody else – means to fight the hardest battle which any human being can fight; and never stop fighting."

But you don't have to battle alone. You can surround yourself with friends and individuals who expect the best. This may mean eliminating time with negative people who love puncturing other's dreams. You don't need a dreary group pulling you down. You want an enthusiastic band of cheerleaders expecting you to reach the peak. Better yet, you want cheerleaders climbing alongside you. Together, you can inspire one another to remain resolute. You can share inspirational stories and emulate those who have scaled the highest mountains.

At the end of 21 days, you will recognize tremendous progress, more than you could ever imagine. Because of the power of expectation.

Accept Victories

If you aspire to the highest place, it is no disgrace to stop at the second, or even the third, place. – Cicero

Small victories are stepping stones toward greater success. Therefore, we must recognize and accept even the tiniest of victories. Otherwise, we'll never appreciate the top of the mountain. Acceptance suggests that we acknowledge exactly where we're at even if we still have a long climb.

If we have difficulty spotting or accepting victories, it may indicate that a self-sabotage program is running in the background such as, "I don't deserve success." Recognizing our saboteur is in itself a victory, for we now have tools for correction. We can forgive ourselves for sabotaging thoughts and take the necessary steps to implant healthier ones.

If we become overly concerned about not healing, achieving or succeeding, we won't notice the little miracles that appear along the path. Acceptance asks that we stay awake to the subtle differences in our thoughts, feelings and behaviors. It may be as simple as realizing that we've started the day in a cheerful mood. Recognition increases faith and confidence and fuels our desire to improve ourselves.

When my two children were growing up, they took great pleasure in periodically measuring their height. When they grew half-an-inch, they announced with great excitement that they were getting taller. In a similar fashion, we can celebrate along the way. We can acknowledge our courage to remain awake in a world that encourages sleep. Victories without effort are hollow and offer little cause for celebration. Overcoming toxic beliefs requires tremendous effort. At the end of the day, we can stand on the ledge and look down the mountain and rejoice at how far we have come. A considerable climb may still lie ahead, but we can be grateful for what we've accomplished.

Gratitude teaches us to appreciate our lessons, the people around us, and the simple pleasures of life, such as fragrant flowers or hot showers. We may want to ride powerful stallions but find ourselves on old mares, yet we can still be grateful we aren't walking. When our minds nurture gratitude, we fill our souls with abundance and are more inclined to extend a hand to others as they climb their mountains.

A mindset of gratitude teaches us to remember our previous successes and to step forward toward the next grateful moment. With a vision of gratitude, we can appreciate even the difficult lessons. We can't ski black diamonds until we have mastered the easier slopes. To skip a training session may be courting disaster. Therefore, we can be grateful for learning the lessons in the order they appear. As the mythologist Joseph Campbell said, "Where you stumble and fall, there you discover gold."

When we're not getting what we think we need, we can return full circle and inspect our lives once again. This will show us where to dig and find gold. If, for example, there's a recurring problem with scarcity, we can unearth the embedded beliefs about unworthiness that need correction. The IRSPEA anti-virus program is meant to be used as an ongoing process of Inspecting, Rejecting, Selecting, Projecting, Expecting and Accepting.

As long as we continue to examine our lives, release our fear-based beliefs, and install new programs, we will clear out the mental debris. The purification is similar to cleaning an aquarium. An efficient filtration system clears out the waste from a fish tank, but after awhile the aquarium needs a thorough cleaning. When the fish are safely removed, we pour clear water into the gravel and release the waste. We then empty the murky water and repeat the purifying process. The gravel gets flushed and the water becomes clear. The fish can happily return to a fresh home.

The same holds true for our lives. If our filtration system is clogged with emotional and mental waste, we can clear out the debris and purify ourselves. Fortunately, the Guiding Power of Spirit helps us heal and break free from destructive thoughts, feelings, and behaviors. The light of Spirit shines brightly and increases our wellbeing. It also prepares us for the next stage of awakening – **Heartbeat of Connection.**

MAPPING EXERCISE

1. Allow some reflective time to complete this exercise. On the left side of your journal, make a list of the wounding beliefs that you have held or still hold about the following areas: your personality, your body, lifestyle, relationships, love, men, women, sex, success, career, money and God. Include those self-defeating thoughts passed down from your caregivers. Then create a list of healing declarations on the right side of the page. Think of ways to incorporate healing declarations every day into your life.

Wounding Thoughts/Beliefs	**Healing Declarations**
My Personality	My personality
My Body	My Body
My Lifestyle	My Lifestyle
Relationships	Relationships
Love	Love
Men	Men
Women	Women
Sex	Sex
Success	Success
Career	Career
Money	Money
God	God

2. **Create a vision board.** Construct a cut-and-paste model or a computer version of your vision board. Choose pictures and words that best represent your declarations, intentions and goals. Incorporate your healing declarations. The collage may display your life purpose as well as aspirations for a partner and family. This is the vision of your future and you are creating it NOW.

If you are in a relationship, consider making a vision board together. It can identify common values, desires and goals. And if you have children, involve them in a family collage to show that everyone has a part in creating community.

GUIDED VISUALIZATION

Imagine a spacious, beautiful garden. This garden has colorful flowers, flourishing trees, and running water. However, there is a barren area choked with weeds. You carry a large burlap sack and move through the garden. You pluck each weed and place it in the burlap sack. Each weed represents an emotional wound that you received, a damaging message from a caregiver, a corrosive thought, or other noxious belief that you picked up along the way. This is a time to pluck each constricting weed and place it in the sack.

The bag gets heavy as the weeds form a pile. Consider the many burdens you've been carrying through life. The heaviness of neglected wounds has been overwhelming. It has stolen space in your life and thwarted your beautiful garden.

Look around and realize that you are not alone. There are other beings of light assisting you, healing you, clearing the field with you. As a matter of fact, each person you encounter in life can help you remove a weed if only you let them. Ask for assistance when you feel overwhelmed. Help is sure to come.

Clear the field and fill your bag. When you are finished, take the sack to a compost pile. All those experiences served a purpose at one time, but now they're ready to be transformed. Bless the compost with forgiveness, knowing you can release and let go. A ray of sun appears and transmutes the strangling weeds into golden seeds of opportunity. Worthlessness becomes a seed of worthiness; poverty transmutes into a seed of prosperity; self-hatred morphs into self-love. These are new seeds of confidence and self-worth, power and success, wealth and prosperity, health and rejuvenation, love and compassion, joy and peace.

Return to the cleared field with the bag of golden seeds. Plant them one-by-one with loving tenderness. The seeds represent new declarations that you have innumerable rights: the right to live in a beautiful garden; the right to water your garden with emotional experiences that bring joy; the right to choose the seeds you wish to grow and nurture; the right to love all the vegetation and receive bountiful love in return. The right to talk to others about your garden and have them listen attentively; the right to display your flowers and plants and have them accepted and recognized as beautiful creations; the right to receive the blessing of Spirit bathing your garden with healing rays of sunshine.

As you plant your seeds, they immediately sprout in your subconscious mind. See them grow. Imagine the field turning lush with vegetation. The stems draw nourishment from the earth and extend it upward to the plants. They form buds that open into beautiful flowers. Your field is ablaze with a canopy of colorful petals of different sizes. Among them is a batch of lilies. They are gifts that remind you that all is forgiven.

You notice a large red flower sprouting in the center of your field. It represents your opening heart. You inhale the beautiful fragrance and your chest expands. A brilliant, healing light pours from the heavens. It flows through the top of your head and expands your heart. Love circulates through your body. The brightness glows. You inhale love and, as you exhale, you feel inner peace. A smile crosses your face and you rejoice. Your mind is now a garden of paradise.

Enjoy your garden now. Walk among the lilies and the other beautiful flowers. See them grow and multiply. Notice that your abundance brings others to your garden. Share freely, for you have so much to give. Pass your flowers and seeds to those who need gentle reminders to tend their own gardens. Your generosity inspires them.

Remember that you can return to this garden as often as you wish. The flowers are there to be admired and shared. You appreciate your role as caretaker and lovingly tend your plants. You gently replace unwanted weeds with beautiful thoughts and joyfully watch your garden flourish.

Collect a bouquet of your favorite flowers and prepare to bring them back to present time. With a colorful display in hand, slowly bring your awareness back into your body. Become aware of your breathing and the lovely scents around you. Gently return to present time with a feeling of love and bounty.

Record the experience in your journal.

CHAPTER SEVEN

HEARTBEAT OF CONNECTION

All who call on God in true faith, earnestly from the heart, will certainly

be heard, and will receive what they have asked and desired.

– Martin Luther

A loving old sage called Jayadratha agreed to teach the ancient wisdom to his new disciple, Sathana, a very eager student. One summer morning, Sathana followed Jayadratha on his morning walk. The wise man's long strides took him along a beaten path next to a winding stream that carved its way through the countryside.

Sathana quickened his pace to catch up with the sage. "Master," asked the student, "How do I discover my True Self?"

Jayadratha smiled at the man and walked on in silence.

They arrived at a place where the water was shallow and still. Succulent figs dangled from a tree on the opposite bank.

"Great Master," repeated Sathana, "How do I find my True Self?"

Again nothing was said as Jayadratha blissfully waded into the stream toward the ripened fruit.

Sathana splashed behind and spoke once more. "Master, please, I want to discover my True Self."

Jayadratha stopped midstream and seized the student by the scruff of his neck. His strong arms pushed the struggling head underwater. Precious seconds ticked by. Finally, he released Sathana who surfaced, gasping for air.

The irate disciple backed away and coughed and sputtered, "Why did you do this?!"

His master eventually spoke. "When your desire to find True Self is as great as your desire to breathe, only then will it come and in an instant."

The next stage of awakening, Heartbeat of Connection, fuels a burning desire to return Home. Now that we have learned to eliminate viruses and install healing software, we are now ready to optimize our computer and increase the processing speed for a faster and clearer connection with our GPS. Spirit regularly downloads updates to show us that Home is the center of our heart.

During this phase, we expand on three powerful principles: *Love, Trust and Self-mastery*. Let's begin with the most important.

Love

A joyful heart is the inevitable result of a heart burning with love. – Mother Teresa of Calcutta

Love is inherent in each of us. We don't have to find it; we merely have to access it. Love is our very essence, our natural state of being. Love has nothing to do with performance or the cravings of ego. It is unconditional, without guilt or shame. It has no boundaries or expectations. It simply unfolds in joyful harmony. Love is all there is and encompasses all that we are.

The comedian Lucille Ball once said, "I have an everyday religion that works for me. Love yourself first and everything else falls into line. You really have to love yourself to get anything done in the world."

Learning to love myself as I am has been an ongoing odyssey. The words of the mystic Rumi clearly apply to me: "Your task is not to seek for love, but merely to seek and find all the barriers within yourself that you have built against it." As I was growing up I erected many barriers around my heart. Now I continually discover embedded wounds and fears that need to come into the light. As Jerry Jampolsky says in *Love is Letting Go of Fear*, "Love is the total absence of fear. Love asks no questions. Its natural state is one of extension and expansion, not comparison and measurement."[1]

When we practice self-love which, again, has nothing to do with ego, we turn the key in our heart and open a door to expansion so that Spirit can more readily flow through us. As we move deeper to our core, beyond the ego and the world's beliefs, we find our center, our True Self, and that is love. This transformative power extends through each petal of a flowering life. It affects the way we relate with the physical home of Spirit and how we feel. It shifts thoughts and teaches us to relate with compassion. Love shapes our communication and our perceptions of the world.

Romantic love would have us look outside ourselves for that special relationship that fills a void. Two empty vessels can be companions, but they cannot fill each other. Over time, each vessel will complain about the emptiness and blame the other for not fulfilling the promise of abundance. However, if each accesses the inner wellspring of love, each can overflow with abundance.

The heartbeat of connection is about loving from the inside out. It means returning to our Source and extending love outwards. Connected to the loving heartbeat, we become instruments playing in a Divine orchestra. We resonate with creation and witness love flowering everywhere – a glorious full moon, a fluttering hummingbird, even a working ant.

Loving from the inside out starts at the center of our heart. It allows us to become more fully who we are. Love awakens the senses, deepens our feelings, expands our mind and allows us to experience and express compassion toward others. With love we recognize that we belong to the same family. We let go of barriers and deepen our trust in Spirit.

Trust

Trust thyself: every heart vibrates to that iron string. – Ralph Waldo Emerson

Trust is an inner knowing that the Guiding Power of Spirit is always with us. It is similar to the trust we have in a navigational system in a car. We don't question whether satellites are orbiting the earth and beaming the correct coordinates. We implicitly trust the information without knowing all the intricacies of navigation, and follow the directions toward the destination.

We are asked to develop that same level of trust in our inner GPS. We must rely on the unseen and the unknown, two qualities that rattle egos which want control. However, when we hear the loving heartbeat, we can rest like a child against a mother's bosom and know that we are safe, protected and loved. We are never abandoned by Spirit.

I endeavor to hold that trust firmly in my heart, especially when it applies to my eternal Home. But my trust is continually tested. Growing up as a self-reliant and independent boy, I learned to be wary of men in authority. The Catholic image of God the Father struck me as someone sitting in judgment. Would I place my trust in a judgmental God who might toss me into hell? Not likely. I had to deepen a connection with a Divine Source who was loving and compassionate. Someone I could trust with my hear and soul as well as material needs such as finances, relationships and health. Because wounds of neglect pierced my young heart, I have to continually nurture the belief that an All-Knowing Spirit is involved in my life on a day-to-day basis. Instead of being that self-reliant man who doesn't need help, I seek to continually ask for assistance from my GPS and place my trust in the Divine.

Whenever I fail to trust, I remember the story of Moses. Even though he witnessed plenty of miracles, he still struggled with his own trust issue. When he was in the desert with the Israelites, there was no water. He was instructed by Yahweh to strike a rock to supply water. Moses struck the rock not once but twice, possibly thinking he needed to get it right or to remind Yahweh to take notice. I often remember Moses whenever I'm flailing away at my own rock.

When I do return to a feeling of sublime trust, I am reminded of my children when they were very young. They trusted me and their mother completely. They didn't have to worry about a roof over their heads or food on the table or whether they were loved. They knew all would be provided.

That same level of trust can be experienced with the Guiding Power of Spirit. We can trust that all situations and experiences help us evolve on our personal journey. We may not know why nor understand how each incident or circumstance fits into the overall story, but with trust we can relax into the knowledge that the All-Providing Source is here and now, guiding us Home. We're merely asked to stay connected to the homing beacon. That requires self-mastery.

Self-mastery
When you are master of your body, word and mind, you shall rejoice in perfect serenity. – Shabkar

Self-mastery requires desire and discipline. The more intense our desire, the greater the energy to propel us forward. Norman Vincent Peale's passionate desire to overcome his inferiority complex led him to master the Power of Positive Thinking. With intense desire we will readily embrace the necessary discipline to stay awake.

Consider that the word "discipline" comes from the word "disciple." We are merely asked to become a disciple of our True Self and master the body, emotions, thoughts, relationships, communication and perceptions. Discipline provides the focus, structure and time needed to regulate and amplify the power of each vehicle which, like a spoke of a wheel, is intricately linked to the heart center.

Through self-mastery we raise our antenna and locate the homing beacon. We fine-tune our receiver and move past the static of negative channels toward the powerful Home channel, which transmits heartfelt love outward and around the wheel of life. The loving energy pulsates through our lives and touches the hearts of others.

No doubt, we will occasionally drop the signal. The material world and the ego pull us away from our Source. Unless we are conscious all the time – which requires tremendous desire and discipline – we forget about the internal signal. Self-mastery fuels the yearning to train ourselves to stay tuned to our loving Spirit.

An accomplished master makes whatever s/he does seem easy. With intense passion and focus, Oprah Winfrey creates a talk show that appears seamless; Kobe Bryant or LeBron James play basketball with unabashed skill; accomplished jugglers flip their clubs through the air with the greatest of ease. Those who master a sport or career draw upon a burning passion as their ultimate motivating force.

When we act out of our highest purpose, which is love, we don't mind spending countless hours in training. I, personally, spend many hours writing each week. There are times I'd much rather play outside. Nonetheless, my passion to convey a message with a book requires organized time to play on the computer's keyboard. I must continually master my ego's impulse to procrastinate, by embracing a greater purpose.

When Abraham Maslow constructed his hierarchy of human needs, he placed self-actualization at the top of the pyramid. He said that a self-actualized person finds wonder, beauty and fascination in all experiences.[2] Such a person realizes self-fulfillment and lives with a higher purpose at the apex of the pyramid. In essence, our training is about accessing the heart of desire and living with such purpose.

A human's resting heart rate ideally ranges between 60 and 90 beats per minute. We're not usually conscious of our heartbeat until we actually check our pulse. There are moments, however, after we have exercised or entered a deep meditation, when we actually feel our heartbeat. Imagine feeling that connection throughout the day.

One of the reasons we don't feel our spiritual heartbeat is that ego assumes the role of conductor and tries to orchestrate our many instruments. The body may bounce with hip-hop while our emotions play the blues. The mind could do the cha-cha while our relationships dance the tango. The expressive voice might boom with rap while vision is lost in new age. With ego as conductor, we'll always be out of tune.

Which brings us back to self-mastery. We can train ourselves to recognize the chaos and discover a loving rhythm in our heart.

This requires a still mind so that we can feel the central loving note. With our lives thus attuned, we can create melodies that touch hearts and souls and band together in a global symphony.

If we are to master our instruments, we must distinguish the sound of Spirit from a cacophony of other noises. A discordant ego wields a terrorizing baton over an inner chorus of guilt, fear and shame. Ego's voice is impulsive and tells us to seek happiness outside ourselves – from relationships, careers, material possessions or ingested substances.

In contrast, Spirit as conductor promotes a harmonious orchestra. It does not wave a wand with threatening hand but rather signals us with a calm gesture and soothing voice. Love is the only melody. And if we play the wrong note, our GPS gently guides us back to the proper tune. Some people "just know" when they're hearing the truth. Others need to continually evaluate the many sounds through repeated trial and error in order to gain confidence and trust.

We have trouble with intuitive guidance when we are caught between the wish to satisfy others' expectations and the desire to live our truth. If a woman lives with an alcoholic husband, she may hear a loving message to stop enabling him but may be frightened about taking a stance against a destructive pattern. When she eventually pays attention to the calming voice of her GPS, she can locate the resolve to take action. Discernment is an ongoing process.

Last year my computer crashed a week before I was scheduled to conduct a seminar. My presentation wasn't complete, and worse yet, I hadn't yet backed up the updated file. I frantically called a technician who came to my place. Unable to repair it on the spot, he told me he had to take my laptop to the shop. My immediate internal impulse was "no." I recognized the feeling and let it rise to the surface. Was it the voice of ego or Spirit? I observed and accepted the message, then realized that the "no" was fear-based and clearly came from a lack of trust. I asked my GPS if it was okay to let the computer go. A green light immediately flashed on the screen of my mind. Taking that as a yes, I felt a wave of peace descend upon me. I could trust the man with my precious files. As it turned out, the laptop was repaired the next day at a nominal cost with no files lost. And he optimized my computer at no extra charge!

This example isn't meant to suggest that I always get green lights. There are moments when I calmly receive flashing red lights on my mental screen that indicate "No" or "Don't go," and amber lights that mean, "Wait; do nothing." Whenever facing a decision, I regularly return to the process of observing, accepting, forgiving, asking, listening and receiving. Messages that resound in a calm, loving voice and emanate peace are the ones I seek. I may not always follow the advice, but countless experiments with trial and error over many years have taught me which choices serve me best.

Discernment helps us tune our instruments to the right note. Once connected to the heartbeat, we can increase the volume and let our Conductor guide us in the sound of music. But first we must fine-tune each instrument.

I occasionally play the guitar and have to tune the strings when they're off key. I establish a note and then slowly turn a tuning knob to the right or left until I have the right pitch. I do that with each of the six strings. We need to do the same with our six instruments: *physical bass, emotional timbre, mental note, relational rhythm, expressive tone,* and *visional vibration.*

As we get attuned, we have to stretch. Guitar strings are stretched to achieve the right key. Stretching is different than struggling. When we struggle, we force. When we stretch, we extend outward from a comfort zone into a place of expansion. As disciples of our True Self, we are asked to take bigger risks and extend ourselves beyond the familiar.

At some point, we'll feel some discomfort and pain, especially if we haven't stretched our muscles in awhile. We don't have to suffer. We're meant to treat ourselves with love and trust our GPS. If we feel pain, it's best to pay attention and ask ourselves whether pain is the result of forcing or of stretching. If we're using force, we can ease the pressure. If we're stretching, the discomfort means we're extending ourselves. Taking courageous risks is uncomfortable yet necessary if we want to expand ourselves. We can honor the discomfort, enjoy the stretch, and appreciate the increased flexibility. The ultimate goal is to restore a natural flow and create harmonics as we tune each of our instruments. Let's explore them one by one.

Physical Bass

> Take a moment and feel your shoulders. Notice if there is any
> tightness. Inhale a loving breath while you raise your shoulders
> toward your ears and maximize the tension. Hold your breath for
> three seconds and say, "I love my body." Then drop your
> shoulders. Repeat that two more times. Notice if you create a
> deeper sense of relaxation every time you lovingly hold your
> breath, stretch your muscles, then let go.

If you repeated this exercise with all your muscle groups, you would release tension, increase the flow of energy, and convey to your body that you're taking loving care of it. If you added sensory stimulation, cardio workouts, purified water, fresh air, nutritional meals, and loving doses of rest and relaxation, you would have a nicely tuned body ready to be of service to Spirit.

Having said that, I don't particularly enjoy cardio-exercise. And if I'm tired, I often resist going to yoga class. I do know, however, that when I neglect my body, I feel sluggish and have more difficulty connecting with my GPS. After I do something physical that gets me out of my mind, I feel more balanced. Many people have the same reaction about visiting the health club – resistance before, relief afterwards. This brings us back to self-mastery and the physical body. *Self Sustainable*

Ilchi Lee, in *Brain Wave Vibration*, writes, "Every living creature possesses a natural healing ability, which is essentially the ability to bring one's body back into equilibrium."[3] Since the brain orchestrates bodily functions, Lee focuses on brain vibration exercises and yoga to increase the energy flow.

Brain research highlights the plasticity of the brain, meaning that new experiences create new neural pathways that change the brain and impact our lives. Dr. Kendra Beal, a Chiropractor in Costa Mesa, California, advises us, "Your brain communicates with the rest of your body by means of the nervous system traveling through the spine. A conscious connection with your body from above, down and inside out empowers you to change harmful patterns that compromise functioning. When you establish a mind-body connection, you notice posture, mobility and breathing, and if the body is 'out of whack' you're more apt to take corrective measures to promote longevity and a quality life."

An integral way to establish the mind-body connection is through breathing, an important tool you can consciously regulate to increase energy and relaxation. Just paying attention to your breath brings awareness to your body and grounds you in the present.

A simple breathing technique is diaphragmatic breathing. Merely place a hand on your abdomen and slowly and consciously inhale through your nose as if you are filling a balloon. You will feel your abdomen rise and expand like a balloon. When you exhale through your mouth, you can feel the balloon completely deflating. While breathing this way for several minutes, think of the word "calm" every time you inhale and the word "relax" when you exhale.

By practicing conscious breathing, you continually tune your body as a holy instrument. As the Buddhist Thich Nhat Hanh says, "Breath is the bridge which connects life to consciousness which unites your body to your thoughts."

Unfortunately, modern life has become so busy that it's hard to catch our breath. With everyday stress, not to mention airborne pollution and chemical toxins, we must pay attention to our physical health. When the body is healthy and flowing with energy, we feel better. Toss in junk food, overindulgence and a sedentary life, and we become sluggish. Therefore, a daily practice of caring for our body increases our ability to heal and connect with Spirit's loving messages. Our GPS may instruct us to improve our diet, get more rest, spend time in nature, eliminate an addictive habit, or visit a health practitioner for treatment. It may guide us to tai chi, yoga, breathing techniques, aerobics, massage, raw foods, health retreats, or other programs that release toxins and tone up the body so we can be in tune.

A strong and flexible body, playing in concert with Spirit, harmonizes our senses. We then hear, see, smell, taste and touch with love.

Emotional Timbre

Stop for a moment and notice how you feel. Can you identify three words (e.g., calm, frustrated, loving, sad) that best describe your current emotional state? If you don't feel anything, you may be stuck in your head. If you're anxious or worried, accept yourself, because at least you're aware of your internal state. And if, at the moment, you're overwhelmed with emotions, don't despair because you can shift your feelings. Breathe in love and let go.

This exercise will raise your awareness of the timbre of your current emotions. Self-mastery requires that we pay attention to a range of feelings, for they provide feedback about our internal world. If we shut down our feelings or become overwhelmed with them, we lose our emotional power. We tend to think we are our feelings – I *am* angry, rather than, I *feel* angry. Once we view them as emotionalized thoughts that can be changed, we can more readily shift them.

David Hawkins in his book, *Power Versus Force*, lists a range of emotions that act like a hierarchy of energy. On the lower rung lies shame and guilt, whereas joy, peace and love reside at the top of the scale. We can consciously shift lower emotions to more uplifting ones. Rather than immediately reaching for bliss and serenity, however, we may have to move from one difficult plateau to another, even if it still feels negative. For instance, if I'm stuck in despair, I can shift to anger to mobilize energy. Out of anger, I can take action and climb to the courageous plateau. From there I can step up to optimism and ultimately to peace. When we consciously shift emotions, we reinforce the belief that we are the masters of our emotions rather than the reverse which most people believe.

Loving acceptance and forgiveness is necessary before attempting any shift. Too often we say, "Don't feel bad." If we feel pain, it's better to acknowledge the discomfort rather than move into suppression or denial. We may have to process a wounding experience due to a rocky avalanche before climbing over the rubble.

An emotional catharsis can help us release blocked energy. Since our bodies record emotional experiences, unexpressed feelings stored for long periods become toxic. When we become emotionally sluggish, we can purge the system with some form of release work. This may occur with a therapist, body worker or a safe group setting like a personal growth seminar. I have benefited from numerous healing workshops that allowed me to release years of grief and anger.

Fritz Perls, the founder of Gestalt Therapy, said there were four major emotional releases: anger, sadness, laughter and orgasm. Each one discharges pent-up energy. After a good shout, cry, laugh or orgasm, don't we feel a little bit better?

When we regularly release emotions, we establish a natural flow of energy. Our society doesn't offer many outlets for us to vent and, unfortunately, we save most of our emotions for one person – a partner. Yikes! In reality, we need several loving environments where we can safely sort through our feelings. This allows us to shift to more uplifting ones like joy and love. Talking with an understanding friend, sharing in a group, or journaling alone are examples of safe outlets.

Given all these outlets, we don't have to brood and ruminate unless we choose to. We can see a comedy and laugh, or attend a horror flick and tremble. We can actually master the craft of tuning in to different emotional states. Years ago, Norman Cousins was diagnosed with a life-threatening illness and was given six months to live. He dealt with his situation by turning to laughter. He watched comedies, read funny books, and focused on laughter which helped him relieve the pain. He went on to live another 20 joyous years. His journey is described in his book, *Anatomy of an Illness*.

The choice is ours. We can play sorrowful tunes or joyful, upbeat ones. We can play solo or in concert with others. And we can always tune in to the Spirit channel. It's available 24/7 with non-stop nourishing songs of peace and love.

Mental Note

> Take a moment and watch your thoughts. Your mind may be replaying what you just read or it may be conducting an internal debate about some of the concepts. Notice if your thoughts are more accepting or critical. Now imagine a time when you felt completely loved. If you flashed back to a beautiful moment, realize that you just steered your mind in another direction.

Mastering the mind doesn't mean we force ourselves to think differently. Rather, we lovingly play our mind like an instrument. We choose the lyrics and the music, then practice. If we miss a note, we return to the difficult part and practice once again. And if we need assistance, we merely ask for help from the Master Teacher. Spirit will get us back on key. Spirit will shift the mind from discordant notes of judgment or confusion to the tunes of love.

Ernest Holmes, author of *The Science of Mind*, said, "Our thought is operated on by a universal creativity which is infinite in its capacity to accomplish. Thus in taking thought we do not force anything, we merely decide what thought to follow."[4]

Mindful awareness of our thoughts, moment by moment, corrects the mind when it drifts. Our minds often wander like an easily distracted child in a toy store, running down the aisles, collecting new gadgets and accessories. As we mature, we learn to narrow our focus, process information, and direct our attention to matters at hand. Any difficulty can be viewed as an opportunity to change our internal narrative, strengthen the will, and change our lives.

To fine-tune our mind, we may be guided to practices like mindfulness, meditation, prayer, declarations, Neuro-Linguistic Programming, hypnosis or other mind-expanding programs. With a focused mind attuned to the heartbeat of love, our thoughts are more forgiving and less blaming, more understanding and less judgmental, more loving and less cynical. Spiritual lyrics flow harmoniously.

Relational Rhythm

> Return to a time when you felt completely loved. Notice how that affects your heart. Breathe into that love and say, "I love myself." Notice your internal response. Now recall an incident when a person betrayed, rejected, abandoned or abused you. Say, "I forgive myself for hurting myself." Notice your internal response. You may react with, "It's the other person that needs forgiveness, not me!" Now imagine seeing that person in a mirror. The face changes and becomes you. Remember the time when you felt completely loved. Send that rhythm of love to your mirror image. Notice your response.

Mastering the relational rhythm is about connecting heart-to-heart. It's about loving without fear or guilt. It's the genuine acceptance of others and caring for their personal and spiritual growth. In *Loving Each Other*, Leo Buscaglia wrote, "A loving relationship . . . is home for one's soul – a place to be ourselves and explore our deepest, inner yearnings, hopes, fears, and joys, without fear of condemnation, rejection, or being abandoned."[5] Relationships help us stay awake, recharge our batteries, exchange information, discharge emotion, and fuel the heart.

Relationships can also create power struggles that prompt us to blame, close down, isolate or become co-dependent. Discord occurs when we project our thoughts and emotions onto others. The saying, "If you spot it, you got it," illustrates that what we see represents the parts of ourselves that we disown. Our projections create separateness. Therefore, if I verbally attack a person, I attack myself.

Mastering relationships is about taking ownership, which moves us from helpless victim to empowered owner. When we own a problem, we can change it. Forgiveness transmutes the toxins of hate and resentment into acceptance and love. Of course, it's often easier said than done. Forgiveness can be difficult when we feel wronged. I remember the time a motorist recklessly cut in front of me and I yelled, "I forgive you, you bastard!"

If we lapse back into our projections, we can return to harmonious notes. Since the person I saw represented me, I had an opportunity to see my own reckless part and forgive myself. Each relationship, therefore, becomes an opportunity for lessons. Some lessons require a brief interlude, others turn into lifelong relationships.

The key is to remain in the heart. If I see love, I receive love. Each person becomes a mirror that shows different facets of me. The person I see is the person I am. If I recognize my natural state of love and extend it outward to relationships, I send it back to myself. When I remember that conflict represents separation, I can consciously practice forgiveness and connect back with my True Self where love flows unconditionally.

Self-mastery in the relational area also involves consciously choosing people with whom we want to associate. We can love without guilt and we can also set personal boundaries without guilt. With an uplifted heart, we can play with like-minded souls who enjoy our kind of music. In that way, we continually surround ourselves with uplifting melodies.

As we establish a loving rhythm, we may be guided to heart-centered experiences. Our GPS may direct us to ongoing relational work. This may include books and/or seminars on relationships and boundaries. It may ask that we increase our knowledge about different personalities so that we can better accept others. One such example is the Enneagram, which is a powerful psycho-spiritual tool that identifies nine personality types and their habitual behaviors.

When we appreciate, accept and love ourselves and others, our heart strums in unison. We can then sing, *We are the World*.

Expressive Tone

> Pause a moment and consider how you normally express yourself. Are you honest and open with others or only with a select few? What does it look like when you communicate with your authentic voice? Can you express your differences with others and still remain connected with them? How do you express your love to others?

Our expressive voice is a beautiful instrument where heartfelt communication can be honestly expressed. Stirring passages and passionate songs spring forth from a connected heart. The artist within entertains and enthralls when tapped into Divine inspiration. Our voices become speakers for Spirit who shows us how to authentically communicate our truth and lovingly listen to others.

However, we must break through inhibitions about self-expression and climb a transformative mountain while we talk the walk and walk the talk. This requires conscious communication whereby we learn to clearly convey our thoughts and feelings and listen to others with the intention to hear their message. This level of communication requires attunement and self-mastery. We must know how to tune in to another person and intentionally express ourselves. As conscious communicators, we avoid the ego's agenda to be in control and we connect with our heart. From that place, we consciously choose how we send and receive information with an intention to reduce separation and increase connection.

Good communicators spend more time listening and less time debating, attacking or defending. When we listen intently to Spirit's voice, we receive instructions in the art of expressing love and compassion. We can then learn to say what we mean, mean what we say, and say it lovingly. Most importantly, we become well versed in saying, "I love you."

If we ask for help, our GPS teaches us to expand our voices. We are not here to merely sing a few lines. We are meant to express our magnificent selves with vocal variety. As we listen to Spirit, we may be inspired to write or act, sing or drum, paint or work with crafts. We may be led to Toastmasters to gain confidence in public speaking or we may be guided to silent meditation so we can listen to our inner voice.

For the past 30 years, my writing has been a significant expressive medium. In my journals, I've worked through inhibitions and revealed many truths. In the process, I have faced both my shadows and my light.

Once we find our own particular medium and establish a heartbeat of connection, we become more receptive to the loving tones of Infinite Intelligence.

Visional Vibration

> Stop for a moment and ponder your life purpose. Are you committed to fulfilling that purpose, no matter what? Does it inspire you to take risks and face your fears? Do your talents serve your purpose? Do you hold a dream so large that it seems impossible? What holds you back? How would your life change if you manifested your grand vision?

Now that we've tuned the first five instruments, we're ready to end on the right vibration. That takes us to vision. When we're connected with our Divine purpose, we incorporate our talents, gifts, and creativity with a vision fueled by love. Inspiration and flashes of genius follow because we've stepped into an infinite ocean.

We all have a Divine purpose. That's why we're here. Ultimately, we are meant to return Home. Along the way, we receive a loving note from Spirit. This directs us to a vocation where we can make a unique contribution. A waitress, conscious of the Divine, can touch the hearts of diners. A teacher can inspire students. A police officer can protect the community.

We are asked to make choices that are Spirit-driven rather than ego-driven. When our ego is in the driver's seat, we choose a career based solely on money, survival or the expectations of others. We squander our talents and resist grand visions. When we are Spirit-driven, on the other hand, we're aware of and embrace our mission on Earth and consciously extend our light into the world. Spirit utilizes our talents and supports our endeavors so we can fulfill our purpose.

Living our purpose may mean that we take time off from busyness so we can turn our eyes inward. Joseph Campbell spent several years living off his life savings to study and research mythology. He wrote extensively about the hero's journey. The word "hero"

comes from the Greek *heros*, meaning "to protect and to serve." The function of the hero is to sacrifice, learn, grow and act for a higher cause or goal.

A heartfelt vision directs us to become heroes and heroines and act in service for the higher good. This doesn't mean we sell everything and move into an ashram. It means we step away from small dreams and let Spirit guide us to the top of the mountain. Many people intuitively "know" what they're meant to do but often they thwart the idea because of fear. Fear can paralyze; it can also motivate. It's the forerunner to courage. And courage is what we need when we commit to a vision.

Viktor Frankl, a psychiatrist who survived Auschwitz but lost his family during the holocaust, wrote the acclaimed book, *Man's Search for Meaning*. He said, "He who has a 'why' to live can put up with almost any 'how.' " That "why" is the meaning or purpose we ascribe to our lives.

When you connect with your GPS, you download the "why." It's the purpose and vision that shows you what you're meant to do. And it's something that only you can do. You may be encouraged to sponsor products and services that heal our planet or promote cooperation in the business world. You may be asked to raise a loving family or inspire a community. You may be guided to change careers or work in a specific part of the world.

Once we receive clarity of purpose, we know that our particular talents and gifts are meant to make a difference in the world. We can then forge a mission that narrows our focus. A mission statement combines vision with action and can pertain to a personal life, family, corporation or community.

One of my first mission statements developed out of a men's retreat: "To create a prosperous and powerful inner and outer kingdom to heal wounded spirits through my words." That has guided me through my work with clients, my writing, and my presentations. Not surprisingly, my current mission weaves those ideas with the principles of this book.

Mission statements keep us on course. If we ever wonder about making a decision, we can always refer back to our mission and ask if the decision furthers our cause. With a clear vision and direction, we can choose that which is in the highest good.

A grand vision allows us to see the purpose behind each encounter. Insight increases our consciousness so that we see the lessons in every opportunity. If we need to expand our vision further, we can attend retreats and vision quests or reflect on our dreams. We can find a coach or spiritual teacher to help us develop our life purpose or we can attend metaphysical classes, sweat lodges, or indigenous rituals that teach us to open the third eye and see past the world of illusions.

Clear about our vision, we can now hold a high vibration.

The table summarizes the attunement of our instruments.

ATTUNING THE INSTRUMENTS

Home Instruments	Attuned	Out of Tune	Ways to Fine-Tune
Physical	I am comfortable with an evolving physical body with awakened senses that interact with the external world.	I am disconnected from my body and the natural world and my senses are shut down.	I awaken my body with yoga, diet and nutrition, exercise, massage, sensual experiences, tai chi, time in nature, or other body modalities.
		OR I am obsessed with my body, addicted to my senses, and overwhelmed by the environment.	**OR** I shift my focus inward through breathing and meditation.
Emotional	I accept and manage evolving emotions that provide feedback about the internal world.	I am cut off from emotions and lack joy.	I connect with emotional states and safely discharge them.
		OR My emotional states are excessive with extreme highs and/or lows.	**OR** I shift toward uplifting emotions such as laughter or joy.
Mental	My inquisitive mind processes information and focuses and directs attention.	I am closed-minded and unable to see my thoughts, mental process, and patterns. I am dogmatic and rigid in my beliefs.	I become aware of my preconceptions and beliefs. I practice mindfulness, meditation, prayer, NLP, hypnosis, or other mind-expanding programs.
		OR My mind is confused and ever-changing and I procrastinate.	**OR** I use affirmations, declarations and intentions.
Relational	My open heart connects with others with compassion and love.	I have a closed heart and experience loneliness.	I practice forgiveness and open my heart. I lovingly connect with relationships and see others as reflections in my mirror. I learn about personality types to accept myself and others.
		OR I am co-dependent and have few boundaries.	**OR** I practice self-love with appropriate boundaries.
Expressive	My voice freely expresses my inner truth.	I suppress my voice and inhibit self-expression.	I express my voice through words, song, or other expressive mediums. I learn communication tools.
		OR I am an exhibitionist with an obsessive need to be heard.	**OR** I practice silence and listen to my inner voice.
Visional	My vision provides insight and guidance. I uncover hidden talents and clarify my life purpose and direction.	I am invisible and my talents and purpose are hidden.	I become self-revealing. I incorporate talents into a vision and create a mission statement. I utilize meaningful rituals to see my vision.
		OR I am grandiose and impose my views on others.	**OR** I meditate and reflect in order to gain insight.

Now that our instruments are well-tuned, we're ready to create song and verse. We harmonize the physical bass, emotional timbre, mental notes, relational rhythm, expressive tone, and visional vibration. With this harmonious orchestra, we can send powerful heartfelt songs rippling through the universe in melodic verse. They become manifest when we synchronize our instruments with the Guiding Power of Spirit and consciously broadcast our melodies. We explore this more thoroughly in the next chapter – **Conscious Creation.**

MAPPING EXERCISE

This exercise requires time to reflect on the questions. They will expand your thinking and lead you to a mission statement.

1. My current heroes are . . . *G Roosevelt mBs*
2. The qualities I admire in them are . . . *altoristic, smotivator, powerful*
3. The values that are truly important to me include . . .
4. My unique talents are . . .
5. The accomplishments I am most proud of are . . . *PhD Thinking*
6. What I most love to do is . . . *home – garden*
7. I feel most at home when I . . .
8. One of my seemingly impossible dreams is . . . *Address unkP*
8. Before I die, I want to . . . *teach healing*
9. If I had one year to live, I would . . . *Travel Spiritual Desti*
10. My grand vision for my life is . . . *to spread peace*
11. I want to become a leader who . . . *inspires*
12. I act in service to my True Self when I . . . *share ideas*
13. My mission statement (vision plus action) is . . .

gratitude, cooperation, integrity, Loving kindness, compassion

GUIDED VISUALIZATION

Imagine yourself resting on the side of a mountain. During the long climb, you experienced challenges and learned lessons. You released many beliefs. You now make your way to the top of the mountain where you find a towering gold pyramid. You search the base of the giant structure, seeking an entrance. None can be found.

You rest against one of the gold walls and spot a giant butterfly with sparkling rainbow wings, fluttering overhead. It descends and whispers to you, "Return Home." You answer the call and clamber up the side of the pyramid.

Near the top there's an opening. You enter a narrow passage and follow a torch-lit path deep into the heart of the pyramid. There, you find a secret chamber. In the center of the room is a gold throne. It sits directly below the apex of the pyramid and beckons you.

You take your place on the throne. Suddenly, all the torches are extinguished. You are surrounded in black. You're not afraid. You are ready to complete the journey. The darkness draws your attention deeper within. You feel the gentle thumping of your heartbeat. The blood of life flows through your body. You breathe into your heart. You and your heart become one.

Feel the beautiful rhythm. The tempo ripples through your body and pulsates with emotion. The doors of your mind open and your throat hums a melodious chord. Your third eye opens. A beam of liquid light drops from the apex of the pyramid onto the crown of your head. This loving light penetrates your mind then enters your heart. Love expands and penetrates every cell of your body. It harmonizes your body, emotions, thoughts, heart, voice and vision.

You undergo a metamorphosis. You shed the skin of ego with all the constrictions and beliefs. You welcome the heartbeat of connection and the light of illumination. Energy radiates from your body. Joy and peace surround you.

The chamber is now flooded with luminosity. It pulsates with the same rhythm. The power of love flows through you. This attunement activates a screen in your mind. A flash of intuition reveals your life purpose. You see a map with your path clearly marked. The path leads you to a house inside a heart. This vision shows the way. It clarifies your mission.

Sitting on your throne, you reclaim your True Self. Divine inspiration guides you to direct your life with a loving heart. Your brilliance bursts forth like a star in the heavens. Whatever you intend becomes manifest. You see your purpose and mission unfold in your mind and it takes form in the world. You are a creator of life.

You glide out of the pyramid and spread your wings. No longer bound by restriction or constraints, you soar from the mountain. High in the sky you reveal the glory of creation to those climbing below.

Your magnificent transformation inspires others to scale the peak. You send them a message, "Return Home."

From your vantage point, you now recognize that the Earth is a giant heart. It beckons you and all of humanity to become stewards of the planet. You accept the call, for you now pulsate with the heartbeat of connection. You are returning Home.

Spend a few minutes and record any thoughts in your journal.

CHAPTER EIGHT

CONSCIOUS CREATION

Every thought vibrates, every thought radiates a signal, and every thought attracts a matching signal back. We call that process the Law of Attraction.

– Abraham (Esther Hicks)

The concept of conscious creation makes me want to create colorful balloon animals. That may be a far cry from manifesting luxurious homes, beautiful relationships, vibrant health, bundles of cash, and inner peace but the same principles apply. It's a matter of playing and creating – consciously.

So let's talk about balloon animals. Before I breathe life into a rubber casing, I have to identify a need, clarify and state my intention, knowing that I have the air to inflate, create and shape rubber into an animal. As I work through any difficulties such as bursting balloons, I allow the creation to emerge and rejoice at the red giraffe or blue teddy bear.

This is an example of conscious creation. Let's explore this concept more fully. The psychologist Gordon Allport said that the intentional nature of individuals unifies the personality as it strives toward achieving goals. When intentions come from the inside and expand outward through the six instruments, we manifest on the material plane.

We are all meant to shine our light into the world. However, this may create tension. As we stretch and grow, we inevitably take more risks and move out of our comfort zones. This generates stress because we are expanding and actualizing our potential. Blowing up a balloon stretches the rubber. We do the same when we consciously breathe into a partially inflated life. We expand our capacity to shape our lives.

Initially, we may be tempted to focus on manifesting objects outside of ourselves. Indeed, some of our creations will require physical support such as homes, vehicles, money and partnerships. Real alchemy, however, takes place on the inside where the fires of truth, courage, trust and love melt old leaden beliefs and transform them into gold.

John Randolph Price offers abundant wisdom about manifestation in *The Abundance Book*. He writes, "My consciousness of the Spirit within me as my unlimited Source is the Divine Power to restore the years the locusts have eaten, to make all things new, to lift me up to the High Road of abundant prosperity."[1] He goes on to say that it's actually impossible to have any needs or unfulfilled desires since we are manifesting exactly what we need to learn.

When we first tune our instruments, we start with basic melodies. Once we become proficient with scales, we expand our repertoire and play more complicated songs. Then, perhaps, we join a local band. If we continually practice and expand our skills, we may take a seat in the orchestra. With the Guiding Power of Spirit as our director, we play as conscious co-creators and intentionality manifest music. We create from the inside out and come from our Source, not from the ego. Intentions that resonate with Spirit seek the highest good and vibrate with love.

As with most of life, there's an unfolding process. Another diagram of a flower with six petals takes us through the stages of conscious creation.

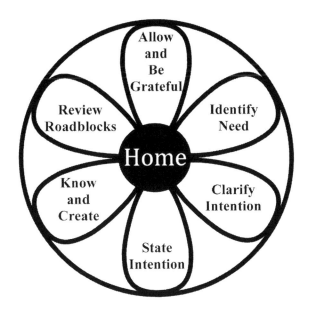

1. Identify Need.

When we want to create something in our life, it usually starts with a need, want or desire. Abraham Maslow listed a hierarchy of needs in the form of a pyramid. Our physiological needs form the base. As we satisfy the need for food, water, sleep and sex, we move up the pyramid to fulfill our need for safety and security. Once we satisfy each level of need, we reach higher up the ladder of human potential. As we feel safe, we climb toward love and belonging, upward to self-esteem, then onto a deeper understanding of the world, upward to beauty and the arts, then finally, self-actualization where we achieve "peak" experiences.

If we are struggling with basic needs, such as wondering how to pay bills, we'll focus our attention there. A self-actualized person has learned how to recognize and satisfy fundamental needs. Therefore, it's important to identify the immediate need calling our attention so we can resolve and evolve. If we're unable to play the musical scales, it's far more difficult to create complex, mystical songs.

We are meant to reach the apex of the pyramid. Hence, we must learn how to consciously shape our lives. Some needs are easy to identify. Money and love are often at the top of the list. They reflect the need to survive and be safe, to belong and be loved. A 40-hour work week and intimate relationships take considerable energy and time.

We may have difficulty identifying other basic needs such as feeling good about ourselves, exercising our power, connecting with others, being heard and recognized, and living a purposeful life. There may be times when we know what we want but are unclear about the underlying needs. We may want a loving relationship but may not be aware of the unmet dependency needs craving attention. When they remain hidden and unfulfilled, a relationship falters. So what may appear on the surface as a control or communication problem may actually represent unmet needs yearning to be acknowledged and satisfied.

Beneath every problem, there's an unfulfilled need. If we enter a supermarket, unsure what we desire, we'll wander aimlessly around the aisles. Then again, if we had previously scoured the cupboard and wrote a list of what was missing, we could quickly fill the shopping cart.

Unearthing a need is the first step in conscious creation. This is not an easy process because many of us have been taught as children to suppress our needs and desires. It that was the case, we can become archeologists and dig beneath the surface by asking ourselves, "What do I need, want and desire in this situation?"

Imagine if we asked that question every day. It would remind us to acknowledge our needs and move up the pyramid. When we ignore our desires, we still create but unconsciously. Awareness moves us inward toward conscious creation.

2. Clarify an Intention.

Once we bring our needs into the light, we can clarify an intention. Clarity requires reflection and sorting through what we want and desire. It's like turning the pages of a balloon manual to decide which animal to create. Clarification shows us what we clearly want as well as what we don't want. Both sharpen our mental image. If we seek an intimate relationship, we paint a picture of the desired outcome. We spell out those attributes we definitely want and those we cannot tolerate. One person may imagine a physically attractive partner who enjoys exercise and exotic vacations while another may visualize a soul mate who shares literature and meaningful conversations.

This very process may raise conflicting beliefs. For example, if I want to manifest love but have an embedded belief that I don't deserve love, I'll experience discomfort and resistance when it comes my way. A conflicting belief reduces the impact of an intention. An unconscious embedded belief trumps a conscious intention. Fortunately, Spirit trumps the unconscious. Its guiding light shines into the dark recesses of our minds so we become conscious.

As we clarify our intentions, we raise our awareness and crystallize our desired goals. We can draw on the principles of IRSPEA (Inspect, Reject, Select, Project, Expect, Accept) to shift internal states so we are congruent with what we desire. This may involve releasing and letting go of our limiting beliefs.

We can hold many intentions. Some may be very personal like health, or they may involve others like a partner, children or customers. We may be tempted to change people rather than ourselves. That is a waste of energy. The only person to change is oneself. The best intentions pertain to changes in our own perceptions and behaviors and seek the highest good. We can ask the Guiding Power of Spirit for help in clarifying the highest good for both ourselves and others. The serenity prayer says it best, "God, grant me the serenity to accept the things I cannot change; courage to change the things I can; and wisdom to know the difference."

Interestingly, the very process of clarifying an intention can materialize it. We might feel a longing for friendships and clarify a desire to open our heart. We might then receive a call, seemingly out of the blue, from an acquaintance who invites us to a social gathering. Spontaneous miracles occur along the journey of conscious creation.

3. State the Intention.

This next step may sound rather simple. If we were encouraged as children to openly express our needs, stating the intention is easy. If we were taught to suppress our voice, then this step may be more challenging.

I think of the many couples I've counseled throughout the years. Some may have known what they wanted but were unable to make clear requests. They may have expressed their needs in a demanding or pleading way or they may have adopted a hopeless resignation that they would never get what they want. They had to learn the art of making clear requests.

Stating an intention is an act of creation. We give voice to a desire and start a chain reaction. I select a picture in the balloon book and say, "I want to make this orange swan." This leads me to take action. If I wanted to embark on something more difficult, like a 20-foot gorilla balloon, it would involve considerable time, perseverance, resources, passion, focus and energy.

Some dreams may appear out of reach. To make them a reality, we must imbue them with power. This is done by first visualizing the outcome, infusing them with love, and then stating them aloud. A powerfully stated intention that actively engages our six instruments will spiral inward to the unconscious and outward into the world. The synergy of our senses, emotions, mental focus, heartfelt desire, expressive voice, and vision establish a magnetic force to powerfully attract our desired outcomes.

When I moved to California, I had to pass two difficult licensing exams. Since California did not have reciprocity with other states, I had to embark on an intense study program to educate myself on areas that were out of my normal clinical practice. However, my intention was crystal clear. I wanted to pass the exams and move to California. To implant the outcome of the impending tests, I occasionally played Spider Solitaire on the computer. After winning a game, I savored the exploding fireworks on the screen and the phrase, "Congratulations, you won!" If an old viral message surfaced in my mind that I wasn't good enough, I pictured my victory in Spider Solitaire. When I finally took and completed the computerized licensing exams, I pressed the button for the results. Amazingly, these were the words that flashed on the screen: "Congratulations, you passed!"

As mentioned earlier, it's important to attune statements of intent with Divine purpose and the highest good. I have witnessed countless stories about conscious creation. They confirmed my conviction that Spirit knows best. While teaching a seminar in

Australia, I listened to a woman relate a story about finding her dream house in the Australian bush. When she lost out on the contract in a bidding war, she chastised herself for not working harder on stating and holding the intention. One year later, a fire swept through the area and destroyed that dream house. Had she purchased it, she would have lost everything.

To hold the highest good, we can conclude an intention with a phrase such as, "I consciously create this or whatever is in my highest good. And so it is." Alternately, we can end with a paraphrase of the Lord's Prayer. "If it be your will, your will be done on Earth as it is in heaven." Or simply, "Thy will be done." The Guiding Power of Spirit knows far better than the ego what offers our greatest lessons and benefits.

4. Know and Create.

When I make a balloon creation, I have no doubt that I can breathe life into rubber and expand it. There's plenty of air. I start with a long balloon and stretch it several times. I fill my lungs and direct my breath into the rubber. It swells with each exhalation. I then mold the balloon into shape. Without air or effort, I cannot produce an animal. This process represents the next stage of conscious creation – know and create.

Knowing is the realization that the Guiding Power of Spirit is like an abundant supply of air, invisible yet ever-present. This inner knowing allows us to rest assured that our lives are in perfect Divine order. Whatever happens is meant to assist us on the climb up the mountain. Knowing permits us to hold onto dreams without desperately forcing an outcome. This is similar to holding a bird. It must be held tight enough lest it fly away, but not too tight lest it be crushed.

When we place our faith in Spirit, we can let go of expectations of a specific end result. Since our GPS knows the best of all possibilities, we merely have to draw upon the guidance and create.

Creating is about directing the mind. Knowing and creating are two forces that act together. One relies on the implicit trust in Spirit, the other relies on our minds to fashion our lives. They are co-creative forces. Without Spirit, our lives, like balloons, could never expand. Without creative energy, the rubber could never transform into a purple dachshund.

We know that the mind creates a vision of the world. What we see is a reflection of our thoughts and beliefs. When we change our thoughts, our perceptions change and our lives and outward circumstances take on distinctive forms. This is no different from shaping balloons. I create a mental picture of an animal and transfer it to rubber. I change the internal image in my mind and produce another outcome.

Knowing and creating asks us to rely on our GPS to guide us as we create through our thoughts. This will test our faith. The impatient ego will insist, "MY will be done," or demand, "I want it NOW!" If we become disconnected from our inner knowing, we experience separation, resistance or disbelief. Should this occur, we can quiet the mind, breathe in Spirit, and know that our GPS always directs us toward our highest good. As *A Course in Miracles* says, "There is no will but God's."[2]

5. Review Roadblocks.

Conscious creation is a process. If we are not getting what we think we want, it may be the result of a lack of clarity or readiness, misperceptions, emotional blocks, disconnection from Spirit, or a necessary delay.

Roadblocks raise our consciousness. They stop us in our tracks so we can shine the light of awareness on our lives and review where we're heading. We may realize that we're traveling in the wrong direction or that we need a rest; that we must take a detour or that we require a guide; that we must dig through negative debris or that we need help. There is always a reason for the delay.

When faced with numerous delays during the move to a new church location, Reverend Sandy Moore at the Center for Spiritual Living in Mission Viejo, California reminded the congregation, "Delays do not constitute denial." Her phrase acknowledged that the manifestation process can be frustrating. However, everything has a purpose under heaven.

In May, 2007 I placed my condo in Chicago on the market. Using my manifesting skills, I projected a move to California in October, 2007. The housing market was horrific, but I believed in the power of intention and my GPS was clearly beckoning me westward. It wasn't until February, 2008 that I received an offer. Excited at the prospect, I found an apartment near the ocean and reserved my new home. At the last moment, my condo fell out of escrow. Needless to say, I was crestfallen. I must confess I gave Spirit a "verbal lashing." I had already given away many of my belongings and was anxious to say, "Westward ho!"

After my temper tantrum, I returned to the practice of letting go of ego's demands, connecting with Spirit and using the intentional tools. Still the condo didn't sell. Deep down, I knew that Spirit had a far better perspective about the correct timing. Delay did not mean sitting idle, so I concentrated on creating, which took form in my writing. As it turned out, the additional time in Chicago allowed me to complete my second novel and begin work on this book.

In the middle of April, 2008, still in the throes of a depressed housing market, I received two offers on the very same day. That helped me negotiate a better price. Then in a wild flurry of activity, I moved mid-May. I found a place far better situated than the previous one. It was near wonderful, spiritual neighbors and a mere ten-minute walk from the beach. If my ego was in charge, who knows what would have happened. Clearly, the Guiding Power of Spirit knew what was best.

Conscious creation can take many years for completion. If we want to be a professional athlete, obtain a college degree, write a bestseller, become a multi-millionaire, or accomplish a major undertaking, we may encounter periodic roadblocks and the passage of time. A teenager doesn't become an adult overnight. A silkworm doesn't achieve moth-hood until it first consumes banquets of mulberry leaves.

As long as we hold onto a vision attuned to Spirit, we will resonate with and attract experiences that move us forward on our quests. My first novel took me eight years to complete. I endured 130 rejections from agents and publishers before I found a publisher. It was my ardent desire and inner belief that pushed me to the top of the mountain. During that eight-year period, my GPS guided me to writing classes, writers' groups, rich experiences worth writing about, and a mentor, Lenel Moulds, who played a pivotal role in the development of my skills.

Undoubtedly, there will be times when we're cruising along on the ship of intention and we will strike a submerged iceberg, such as a deeply embedded negative emotion or belief. Those hidden ice blocks reveal themselves so that they can be dissolved and released. When we raise our consciousness, we heal ourselves and melt the frozen beliefs so our ship can continue on its course.

6. Allow and Be Grateful.

Once we've uncovered our needs, clarified an intention, stated it, incorporated knowing and creating, and reviewed roadblocks, we are ready for the final step in conscious creation. We allow our desires to manifest and we receive them with gratitude.

The concept of allowing teaches us to consciously allow what we project outward. Whatever we send out into the world returns back to us. That which we sow, we reap. However, if we believe we are undeserving and have difficulty receiving, we will push away a cornucopia of blessings and manifest scarcity. Therefore, it's important to continually look for evidence that our requests are being answered and to be thankful for the gifts. This maintains the momentum of deliberate creation.

Allowing requires that we continually shift our thinking to the uplifting emotional states we wish to experience. If we desire a fulfilling career, we allow any steps toward that fulfillment to come our way and rejoice when they appear. If we seek financial prosperity, we thankfully welcome each small coin that drops into our lap. If we ask for love, we notice every passing smile and smile back with loving appreciation.

The teachings of Abraham state that allowing is "The state of alignment with the Well-Being that flows from Source. . . . Allowing is deliberately giving your attention only to that which causes a vibration of alignment with Source. When you are in the state of allowing, you always feel good."[3]

We feel good when we're connected to the Source working through our six petals to help us manifest our intentions into blossoming flowers. Plugged into our GPS, we shift our five senses and our emotions to resonate at a higher frequency of appreciation. We consciously think, relate, communicate and perceive in such a way that even a small animal balloon is embraced with playfulness and joy.

A mindset of gratitude takes us higher up the pyramid of human potential. Every thankful step, small though it may be, reduces the distance between an intention and the desired outcome. Many such steps lead to peak experiences. Along the way, we expand our faith and trust, self-confidence and personal power.

Conscious creation is a deepening, unfolding process that takes us inward. If we are not getting what we desire, we can return full circle to identify our needs and wants. Our GPS helps us stay connected with the highest good and opens doors to amazing miracles. They may occur in our health, relationships, career, finances and spirituality. People will come forward to assist us as Spirit marshals support. We no longer have to walk alone. The Guiding Power of Spirit is with us forever, ready to take us to the last chapter in our awakening story: **Homecoming and Inner Peace.**

MAPPING EXERCISE

This exercise is designed to move you through the process of conscious creation. Complete the following steps.

1. What do you need, want or desire? Think of physical, emotional, material, financial, relational or spiritual outcomes.

2. Clarify your intention. Sketch out what you want and don't want. Be bold and specific as you create that which you desire.

3. State your intention. Imagine all your instruments – the senses, emotions, mind, heartfelt love, voice and vision playing together as you visualize the desired outcome. Then read your intention aloud and end with a phrase such as "I consciously create this or whatever's in my highest good. And so it is."

4. Breathe in Spirit and know that your GPS is directing you toward your highest good. Having expressed your desired intention, you have started a chain reaction. Make a list of the ways you can shape your life to create a successful outcome.

5. Review potential roadblocks. Record any hurdles or obstacles that might prevent you from creating what you desire, such

as procrastinating or feeling unworthy or incompetent. Counter each roadblock with a healing remedy such as asking for help, affirming yourself, gaining knowledge, etc.

fit

6. Allow and be grateful. Allow yourself to experience the senses and emotions of a conscious creator connected with Spirit. Notice how you might think, relate, communicate and perceive. Write a list of the desires you have already manifested. Expand the list to include aspects of your life for which you are grateful.

The following visualization is meant to reinforce your intention.

GUIDED VISUALIZATION

On the screen of your mind, create a special place. This is a room of conscious creation. It's a laboratory where your inner genius can invent and create. This room may be a library filled with books, a studio surrounded by art, a concert stage encircled by instruments, a laboratory housing experiments, or a grotto situated in nature. This is your special place to consciously play and create. Imagine the perfect setting. Then find a space for contemplation.

Now imagine a large oscillating fan above your head. There are six blades, each with a different color – red, orange, yellow, green, blue and purple. They are spinning at the same speed as your thoughts. As a matter of fact, your thoughts provide the power to propel the fan. Notice the rhythm of the rotating blades. As your thoughts move quickly, so does the fan. If you move into a state of relaxation and inner focus, the blades slow down.

In your hand you have a dial that regulates your thoughts and the fan. By turning the knob to the left, you can lower the speed of your thoughts. There are ten settings. Turn the knob slowly to the left, from the tenth setting down to one. You dial back any worries and concerns, and the blades reduce their rotation. As the fan slows, you move deeper within yourself. Feeling calm and relaxed, you allow your inner genius to appear. This is the part of you that loves to create. The genius wants to dream something grand in your life. It may be personal, health related, financial, relational or spiritual. Picture that creation. Let the image become so clear that you know exactly what you want.

In this special room, you have all the knowledge and equipment you need to make your dream a reality. You have a strong body, powerful emotions, a focused mind, a loving heart, a resounding voice, and a purposeful vision. You also have intuition, determination, courage, resources, and, of course, the Guiding Power of Spirit. You draw on these to assist you in manifesting your dream.

Concentrate on your intention or vision. As you hold that intention, you notice that each blade in the overhead fan transforms into a brilliant individualized color. A red blade showers you with a dazzling red light that awakens your senses. You smell, taste, touch, hear and see that which you wish to create. Breathe in red and infuse your body with these powerful sensations.

The next blade on the fan is orange. It beams a dazzling orange light into your body. Your emotions awaken and you feel powerful, courageous, confident, loving and happy. You feel as if you've successfully manifested your dream. Breathe in orange and allow the joyful emotions to permeate every cell of your body.

A yellow blade then sends a radiant shower of light around you and awakens your mind to new possibilities. Your thoughts act like laser beams creating an enormous holographic picture of your dream. Breathe in yellow and allow the luminous light to penetrate your brilliant mind.

Now a green blade pours loving light into your heart. Breathe in the green light and allow your heart to swell with love. The light infuses your intentions with the vibration of love. Embrace your loving self and all that you create.

The next blade is blue. It drops glittering light around you. Breathe in the blue and amplify your voice. You speak your truth and share your magnificent dream. The world hears about your beautiful creation and echoes words of praise.

The last blade on the fan is purple. It envelops you with a healing light that penetrates your third eye. You receive illumination. Breathe in purple and allow your intuition to expand. It guides you toward completion and your highest good. The world rejoices.

Allow the rainbow of colors to flood your very being, into the very cells of your body. The colors surround you with a rainbow bubble that expands your senses, emotions, thoughts, heart, voice and vision. Feel the love and strength pulsate through you. Spirit is with you always and sends you love.

Release your bubble into the world, knowing that whatever you send out, you create. Let your intentions become manifest for the highest good. And so it is.

When you're ready, in your own time, move back to the present.

Record any thoughts in your journal.

CHAPTER NINE

HOMECOMING: INNER PEACE

You are as certain of arriving home as is the pathway of the sun laid

down before it rises, after it has set, and in the half-lit hours in between.

– A Course in Miracles

In Frank Baum's *The Wizard of Oz*, Dorothy yearned to return home to Kansas. After a long transpersonal ordeal, Dorothy is asked by Glinda, the good witch of the North, what she learned. Dorothy responds, "If I ever go looking for my heart's desire again, I won't look further than my own back yard." She realized that home was in the heart. Dorothy also discovered that she could transport herself to that place of love merely by clicking her ruby slippers three times and thinking to herself, "There's no place like home." This brought her back to Kansas where she was lovingly welcomed by Auntie Em and Uncle Henry.

The cast of characters who played the parts of the Scarecrow, Tin Man, Lion and Wizard entered the scene and Dorothy excitedly told them they were also in Oz. Everyone chuckled. Auntie Em informed her it was all just a dream. Dorothy adamantly shook her head and said that the place was real. Still they didn't believe. But it didn't matter because Dorothy was overwhelmed with joy. She was back. In the emotional final sequence, she said, "I love you all," with childlike innocence and then, once again, reiterated her famous line, "There's no place like home."

The credits roll and the audience breathes a collective satisfied sigh. In the end, Dorothy's transformational arc demonstrated that we all could return home from a long, difficult journey merely by taking action (clicking shoes) and correcting our mind. Action plus thought can create a powerful outcome.

However, did you ever wonder why Dorothy had to leave the colorful world of Oz as portrayed in the movie and return to Kansas depicted on the screen in black and white? And what about the fact that no one believed her? Didn't that seem odd? After all, they were her loving caretakers and friends. Yet, they acted as if Oz was a bad dream and Dorothy would soon get over her childish notion. The ending left the audience to ponder, "*Was* Oz really a dream?"

These puzzling questions, as well as the realized lessons and joyous recognition of returning home, take us to the final phase of awakening – Homecoming: Inner Peace. In this stage we welcome *Celebration, Childlike Innocence, Abundance, Faith, Inner Peace* and a *Home Team.* We also encounter black-and-white thinking and skepticism from well-intentioned friends and loved ones who are not awake. To face those challenges, we incorporate the many attributes of Homecoming.

Celebration

The more you praise and celebrate your life, the more there is in life to celebrate. – Oprah Winfrey

When we complete the long climb up a mountain, we need a celebration. It acknowledges courage, conviction and perseverance. After all, it took incredible effort to wake up and stay awake, follow a roadmap into the unknown, look for signs, heal wounds, break free from limiting beliefs, connect with a loving heartbeat, and consciously create a new way of being. Whew! That requires a *grand* celebration.

How do we celebrate? Consider the long distance runner who crosses the finish line. The crowd erupts in a victorious roar.

The exhausted runner immediately catches her breath and realizes her glorious achievement. She shrieks with joy then collapses into the waiting arms of a throng of companions and loved ones. Joyful tears stream down her face. The endurance race is finally over! She graciously accepts the applause and accolades, then she parties.

Each day can be viewed as a long distance race. Twenty-four hours can seem like an eternity or can pass by in a flash. When we celebrate even the simplest of moments, our lives take on greater meaning. Of course, when we do accomplish something great, we must party.

I had planned to celebrate my 60th birthday living in California. Because of the roadblock of the delayed sale of my condominium, I knew the big move would occur later. I was disappointed because I had long visualized a birthday bash at the home of my sister, Marilyn, and her husband, Bob, who live in Southern California. Then it dawned on me: I could still celebrate. With my sister's help, we organized a festive event. I flew in and partied with family, friends, and even people I had never met. The celebration invigorated me and created a bond with my new location. It also provided the impetus during my final six months in Chicago to muster the energy, perseverance and organization to relocate. After all, I was saying goodbye to a private practice, loving friends, and a way of life, very similar to Dorothy when she received her grand send-off from Oz.

Many of us have endured difficult climbs and have risen from valleys of darkness. We may have overcome health problems, relationship troubles, or personal and financial devastation. Yet we persevered, overcame tremendous obstacles, and learned to believe in ourselves.

We may arrive humbled and exhausted, breathing from an oxygen canister, or we may reach the top with arms pumped high in the sky. But along the way, it's important to catch our breath and applaud our ongoing effort. We can admire our progress and shed tears of gratitude. We can high-five other companions at each plateau and raise our arms high in glorious salute. At any time during our climb, we can always melt into the comforting arms of the Divine and celebrate Homecoming.

Childlike Innocence

Unless you change and become like little children, you will never enter the kingdom of heaven. Therefore, whoever humbles himself like this child is the greatest in the kingdom of heaven. – Matthew 18:1-4

This statement by Jesus clearly portrays the importance of returning Home as children. Innocent children overflow with imagination, wonder, spontaneity, trust and love. They know neither shame nor guilt. They delight in their bodies, are at ease with emotions, have inquisitive minds, and live in the heart. They express themselves freely and are naturally creative. And children know how to party. They giggle and laugh and play with abandon.

A child who lives in the moment recognizes beauty. S/he may stare wide-eyed at the twinkling stars, color a picture with single-minded intensity, snuggle into a parent's arms, delight in blowing bubbles, and have an unwavering belief in the Divine.

Homecoming embraces those childlike qualities. We set aside an inflated ego and joyfully embrace our rightful inheritance of innocence and love. The character of Dorothy embodied those same qualities. When she inadvertently tossed water on the wicked witch, her first inclination was to apologize. She was ever so loving and trusting. And that's one of the reasons we cheered her along the yellow brick road.

The Chinese sage Quan Yin reminds us, "As children do not judge, nor do they intend harm, loving kindness is always easiest to express to them. Learning from this experience, one can begin to treat each other as if he was a child."

When I feel connected with Home, my inner child comes out to play. I recently walked along the beach and spotted a pod of dolphins. I quickly joined a group of strangers by the water's edge. Like little children, we excitedly pointed at the dolphins cresting the waves and shouted many "Wows." We joyously shared our delight over the beautiful creatures. Rather than fear, there was wonderment.

Homecoming teaches us to look upon others with such innocence. We recognize the light within and in others. Strangers are friends in waiting. Holding firmly onto that light brings us back Home.

Abundance

The Spirit within you is forever thinking thoughts of Abundance, which is its true nature. – John Randolph Price

Abundance is a state of mind. We can be prosperous in health, finances and relationships. However, the deeper meaning of abundance is the inward state where, no matter what happens on the outside, we feel bountiful. How could we not feel bounty when we're connected to an unlimited Source? Our Homecoming showers us with abundant love and inner peace. We realize that money or material possessions are not the sources of inner peace. Instead, we appreciate them for what they are, conduits to supply us with resources and experiences to further our growth.

That awareness prevents us from returning to the ego's belief in scarcity, for we are surrounded by abundance. We can discover the little things that bring joy and happiness – a hot shower, a well-stocked library, caring friends, a loving pet, laughing children. We each have our own list of simple pleasures that create the feeling of abundance.

My first experience with real abundance occurred when I lived in Australia. The temperate climate that contrasted with Chicago's harsh winters made me think I was on a perpetual vacation. In addition to the opulence of the surrounding natural environment, I learned about generosity from the Australian people. Even though I wasn't a citizen, the Aussies made me feel right at home. I learned that abundance could be found anywhere in the world. My task was to spread the wealth.

Consider Dorothy. She was ever so generous, not looking to take but rather to give. Even though she was homeless, she overflowed with love and compassion, offering a hand to those in need. And when she returned to Kansas, she radiated those same emotions even when others didn't believe her. She could have easily moved into confrontation, but, instead, she focused on the abundant love swelling within.

Whenever we feel pulled into separateness through conflict, we can follow Dorothy's example and embrace the abundance within and send it outward. Tithing is an example of sharing abundance. As Edwene Gaines writes in *The Four Spiritual Laws of*

Prosperity, "Tithing is a beginning discipline in giving and receiving. It increases our faith and pushes us through conscious fear. When we tithe, we give back to the universe."[1]

Whenever we give of our time, money or resources, we practice abundance. After all, the Guiding Power of Spirit sends us abundant love. We never have to worry about power outages. That's because we have faith.

Faith

Whatever the exact route, the road will be paved with faith – the faith that you have all the resources necessary inside of you to move forward. – Toby Estler

Dorothy maintained a single-minded devotion to return home. She despaired at times but, in the end, her faith was rewarded. The same applies to our Homecoming. Abundant love helps us lock onto the Homing beacon and draw upon an unshakeable belief in the Guiding Power of Spirit.

Faith allows us to let go and let our GPS guide. We rest in the knowledge that decisions can evolve naturally, easily and effortlessly if we welcome assistance. Practicing the art of surrender teaches us to let go of our ego. When we drive off course, we can open our minds and hearts and ask for guidance. At times, we may become impatient, but once we lock onto the beacon, our faith expands. We learn that with every setback, there is a Divine purpose.

Faith teaches us to fine-tune the channel and listen for loving guidance. The ego may resist, falsely believing it has given up free will to some outside spiritual force. Faith recognizes that we willfully choose to spend more time at Home. Who, in their right mind, would want to wander as an orphan, forever lost, when we can rest in exquisite peace?

Every day my faith is tested. I am pulled like everyone else to earn a living, accomplish tasks, maintain relationships, and sustain my body. I feel more comfortable actively choosing and I get impatient when stuck in a project. I have to repeatedly remind myself to let go, ask for help, and realize that the Guiding Power of Spirit has not abandoned me. Spirit does not need reminders to pay attention. Rather, I need constant reminders to have faith.

Homecoming is about taking regular leaps of faith. We may not know why we're asked to visit a particular place or speak with a specific individual, but every time we follow our internal GPS with an act of faith, we strengthen our connection to Spirit and discover inner peace.

Inner Peace

Nowhere can man find a quieter or more untroubled retreat than in his own soul. – Marcus Aurelius

Homecoming is the realization that we can rest at peace in the comforting arms of the Divine. There is no need to rush around and manage life. All that we need is already here. As we increase our consciousness, everything seems to fall into place. Worries fade and forgiveness and love replace judgment and criticism. Our emotions calm, our heart opens, and we breathe love. We get to taste paradise here on Earth.

When my children were little, they'd wake up on the weekend and climb into bed with me and their mother. We'd snuggle as a family and experience tremendous contentment. After replenishing ourselves with emotional sustenance, we'd prepare to begin the day. Those peaceful moments fueled the soul.

Recently, I awoke one Saturday morning in a similar state of bliss. I had finished a week of writing and was in a wonderful space. A feeling of warmth ran throughout my body. Without worries or cares, I felt cared for and loved. It was such an exquisite experience that I didn't want to leave the bed. I turned on my side and spotted a frame hanging on the wall. My daughter had presented me a gift of mounted pictures of smiling Buddhas that she had seen while traveling around Asia. I smiled back at the Buddhas. I could have remained there forever. Then I remembered my yoga class and my next chapter and a few other tasks that beckoned me.

On that morning, I chose inner peace and let the decisions evolve naturally and effortlessly. I felt a gentle nudge to get ready for yoga. I followed the peaceful state that guided me out of bed toward my yoga class. The rest of the day flowed and I noticed synchronicities everywhere. Phone calls and chance encounters all seemed to echo messages about peace. My senses were magnified and it all felt sublime. Unfortunately, that moment didn't last forever. However, whenever I experience such inner peace, it feels like forever.

Even with the uncertainty of life, we can achieve that inner peace. Outside conditions or possessions may provide comfort and a false sense of security, but they do not create lasting peace because we know they can be taken away in a flash. Peace within, however, is everlasting. It is a place where we feel love rather than fear, contentment over worry, openness rather than judgment, and gratitude over want. When we're in that space, we remain peaceful even when stumbling over fallen rocks. The Dalai Lama tells us, "If you have inner peace, the external problems do not affect your deep sense of peace and tranquility."

Dorothy understood that if she ever went looking for her heart's desire, she didn't have to look further than her own back yard. We can follow her example. We can earn a living, raise a family, achieve goals, establish social networks, and still remain at Home. Staying at Home means living consciously with love. Inner calm returns when the awareness of Spirit permeates our lives moment-to-moment, whether we drive a car, visit a friend, or text a message.

If we lose our way, we can correct our course through forgiveness. A forgiving mind is a peaceful mind. With that attitude, inner peace expands outward so that the senses resonate with bliss, the mind focuses on stillness, emotions act in harmony, relationships become loving, communication flows honestly, and purpose unfolds with direction. We merge into Oneness.

A sublime inner calm demonstrates that Home exists in the now. When problems arise, we can recognize the hidden treasures behind each obstacle. Inner peace allows us to turn difficulties into opportunities and, in the process, connect with others at an authentic, soulful level. As our lives evolve miraculously and peacefully, we are drawn toward community.

Home Team

Our chances for Everyday Greatness increase when we surround ourselves with a team and network of other strong individuals – Stephen Covey

Even though Dorothy was on a mission to reach Oz, she found the time to stop and help someone – even a cowardly lion whose initial intent was to frighten her and her companions. Each of Dorothy's encounters became an opportunity to assist and befriend. She embraced diversity which included a silver tin man and a raggedy scarecrow. In the process, she created a community of companions linked together by a common mission.

Dorothy's story suggests that we're not meant to travel alone. Though our internal guidance is personal, we are interdependent and interconnected beings. Spirit resides in everyone and everything and, therefore, love permeates all. When we see the Divine in others, we recognize, "You are me and I am you."

Homecoming teaches us to connect with other souls, to recognize the purpose of these meetings, and experience heartfelt exchanges. We consciously create sacred encounters when we ask, "How can we help each other?"

We then join other companions as part of a wake-up brigade somewhere over the rainbow. Like Dorothy, we connect with unanimity of purpose to renew the mind, strengthen courage, and find heart. We establish a Home Team – a community of like-minded individuals held together by a sense of belonging.

Most sporting teams perform at a higher level in their own field. They are comforted by familiar surroundings and cheered by their fans. We can experience the same with a team linked together by a common belief and purpose. The importance of such groups was presented in Napoleon Hill's *Think and Grow Rich*. He described the Master Mind as, "Coordination of knowledge and effort, in a spirit of harmony, between two or more people for the attainment of a definite purpose."[2] A Mastermind group creates a dynamic synergy more powerful than one mind. It harnesses that power to overcome major obstacles.

I have participated in Mastermind groups for self-improvement, prosperity, writing and spiritual advancement. Each one helped me accomplish more than I could ever achieve on my own. As a matter of fact, this book was birthed through a process of sending out chapters to a Home Team who reviewed them and offered constructive feedback through a series of teleseminars. I sometimes groaned at hearing some suggestions, not because of their critical nature, but because these astute comments forced me to labor further on revisions when I thought I was ready to deliver a chapter. As most women will testify, giving birth is not an easy process. It sure helps when a supportive team assists with the delivery.

Imagine if you were connected to a group committed to returning Home. The impact would be life-changing. You would begin to resonate with a community of individuals who consciously extend love outward and relate on a soul level, whether it be face-to-face or via phone or Internet. Your team would encourage, support, challenge and celebrate one another and contribute to each other's highest good. You can create such a team. All it requires is the desire and a willingness to extend your hand like Dorothy.

When I moved to California, I knew the importance of establishing a vital network. I joined several organizations and created Mastermind groups to satisfy a number of needs including writing, personal growth, spirituality and business. These associations provide regular sustenance and support. I know more connections will follow, for my GPS will direct me to the right people. When the student is ready, a class forms.

It is essential that we find our class, our community. One light brightens a room; many lights brighten a house. You will need other light bearers around you, especially when others try to extinguish your torch.

Facing those who remain asleep

Doubt whom you will, but never yourself. – Christian Bovee

When Dorothy woke up in black-and-white Kansas, the colorful world of Oz had disappeared. Her aunt and uncle, as well as the farm hands, were grateful to have her back. Though they were well-intentioned, they remained in black-and-white thinking and couldn't fathom another world.

Have you ever encountered anything similar when you shared your spiritual journey? When family and friends acted as if you received a nasty bump on the head from a tornado? No matter how you explained it, you encountered glazed eyes or an ensuing debate. Skeptical friends believed that you were the one having the dream rather than the other way around. Yet, deep within your heart, you knew the truth.

The hero/heroine must return from the non-ordinary world. The challenge is to bring Home into the ordinary world, and in the process create an extraordinary life. They must not only alter their own perceptions of what once was but also inspires others to transform the way they see the world. Some will follow the lead; others will remain asleep.

Dorothy's solution was to love others just the way they were. We can easily be pulled back into our egos but if we draw upon the resources and tools that we have learned, we can return inward, recapture the love, and send it out to any discordant mind. That maintains the loving connection with Spirit.

Our interactions with the world then become a dance. We can watch ourselves judging and engaging the ego. We also can step back and observe ourselves with a forgiving mind. We can activate our inner light, smile, send the light outward, and watch the dance floor shimmer with the reflection of love.

Dancing, or any skill for that matter, requires practice. Staying Home is no different. An ongoing spiritual practice in a meditative space can help us strengthen the connection with our GPS. It may be a tiny area in the home or outside in nature. Early morning or evenings provide wonderful moments to meditate, pray, exercise or perform whatever practice calls us to regularly tune in to Spirit.

Consider this practice as similar to the way we would build a relationship with a friend. If we spoke once a year, trust and openness would be hard to sustain, whereas if we talked daily with that friend, we would expand and strengthen the relationship. Any time we set aside for Spirit deepens the relationship. We can send a message to our GPS with a short prayer or affirmation such as, "I expand my consciousness of Spirit in my body, my emotions, my mind, my relationships, my communication, and my perceptions and vision, and I inspire others to do the same."

Remember to involve the Home Team. Without her other-worldly companions, Dorothy might have forgotten about Oz as she immersed herself in the mundane activities of the family. A Home Team reminds us to stay connected while we cycle once again through the stages of awakening.

Circular Process

And the end of all our exploring will be to arrive where we started and know the place for the first time. – T.S. Elliot

Awakening is a circular process. This means we spiral through the stages repeatedly but, with each repetition, we move inward toward the center as demonstrated in the diagram.

We find ourselves at some point adapting to the world again and losing our way. We become orphans once more and are re-minded through wake-up calls to stay awake. We discover additional wounds that need healing so we can break free from deeply embedded beliefs. We experience the heartbeat of connection and return back Home to inner peace. We continue spiraling through the stages, learning new lessons until we rest in the comforting arms of the Divine.

Repetition brings familiarity. The terrain becomes more rec-ognizable so we can climb the mountain with less judgment and more forgiveness, even when we get stuck on an overhanging rock. We can more easily spot the signposts that assist us in the awaken-ing process. With our increased awareness, we strengthen our con-nection with our GPS and recognize Homecoming moments.

The table reviews the cycle of awakening with the description, purpose, lessons and gifts of each stage.

STAGES OF AWAKENING

Stage	Description	Purpose	Lessons	Gifts
Adaptation	We adapt to the material world by downloading society's thoughts and beliefs about the body, emotions, mind, heart, voice, and vision.	To experience the worlds of sensation, feelings, thoughts, relationships, expression, and perception.	Learn about limitation and constriction.	Limitation provides fertile ground for learning, growth, and expansion. (Seeds are planted underground.)
Becoming an Orphan	We move furthest away from Home and forget about the Guiding Power of Spirit.	To extend outward into the world and experience separateness and individuation.	Realize the impact of separation. Learn about excessive and recessive states of imbalance.	The orphan gives birth to the longing for love and connection. (Seeds germinate in darkness.)
Wake-up Calls and Signposts	We receive constant reminders that we have lost our way as well as signposts that provide direction.	To wake up and realize the dream is not reality. To understand the signposts.	Learn to respond to the wake-up calls and read signposts.	Spirit is ever-present and continually calls us Home. Signs are everywhere to guide us. (Rainfall waters the seeds.)
Staying Awake	We learn to stay awake by becoming more conscious of our lives and by asking the Guiding Power of Spirit to keep us awake.	To increase awareness of sensations, feelings, thoughts, relationships, expression, and perception. To become committed to pay attention.	Learn to Observe, Accept, Forgive, Ask, Listen, and Receive. Recognize resonance and dissonance.	Expanded consciousness reveals our True Self and our connection with Spirit. (Plants pierce through the soil and rise toward the sun.)
Healing Wounds and Breaking Free	We clear out the mental viruses and outmoded beliefs pertaining to the body, emotions, mind, heart, voice, and vision.	To heal wounds and break free from old programming.	Learn to Inspect, Reject, Select, Project, Expect, and Accept.	Out of our deepest wounds come our greatest gifts. Forgiveness heals all. (When we clear the weeds, the plants flourish.)
Heartbeat of Connection	We strengthen the heartbeat of connection with our GPS. We become conscious creators.	To expand love, trust and self-mastery with the six instruments to harmonize with Spirit. To discover talents, incorporate them with a life purpose and mission, and manifest the vision into the world.	Learn to fine-tune the instruments and clarify purpose and vision. Learn to Identify Needs, Clarify and State Intentions, Know and Create, Review Roadblocks, and Allow and Be Grateful.	A loving heart harmonizes with Spirit. Our unique talents and life purpose benefit the world. (Ongoing care – nutrients, water and sunshine – creates healthy plants.)
Homecoming: Inner Peace	We return Home to love and inner peace.	To remain connected with our GPS and practice staying Home.	Learn about Celebration, Childlike Innocence, Abundance, Faith, Inner Peace, and a Home Team.	Our natural inheritance is childlike innocence, abundant love, and inner peace. Miracles occur every day. We find community. We are all One. (Plants flower; trees bear fruit.)

It's important to remain patient as we cycle through the stages, just as we would with a child learning to crawl or with an adolescent learning to drive. The latter may require exceptional patience and understanding, but we recognize that each phase has its own unique lessons and gifts. We may stay longer at some phases and speed through others, but we will eventually come full circle and know that we are never away from Home.

It seems fitting that I also come full circle with a final reflection on my childhood. I am forever grateful for that fateful visit to Mooseheart back in 1957, when my quest to find home was born. I have wandered aimlessly as an orphan and endured many steep climbs up difficult mountains. In the process, however, I discovered a roadmap and an amazing GPS.

The Guiding Power of Spirit teaches me to celebrate each day, hold onto childlike innocence, and appreciate abundance all around me. Spirit also reinforces my faith in a greater purpose to all of life. I am alone only when I forget who I am – my True Self. Though I face the modern-day challenges of earning money, meeting deadlines, and paying bills, I can welcome inner peace. With the support of a Home Team, I can walk a spiritual path while connected with fellow soul travelers.

My GPS directed me to Southern California. The right people appeared at the right time to direct me to a community near the ocean. During my search for a place to live, I came across the advertisement for my building complex. It read, "Home at last by the seashore." The library across the street provided another signpost for my new home. I would live in a nurturing place with access to books for pleasure and research, a soulful community, and an ocean to play in. I had, indeed, come a long way since Mooseheart.

To celebrate my move, I purchased a large wooden plaque with an engraved word, "Home." It hangs above the door to my balcony which faces an open park. Whenever I admire the view, the little boy inside of me breaks into a wide smile because he's home at last by the seashore.

My final message is that we are never alone on this magnificent journey. Countless souls are awakening, triggering mass consciousness on a grand scale. As we join the swelling numbers emerging from the dream, we witness the glorious sight of fluttering wings of freedom.

Martin Luther King, in his final speech at the Lincoln Memorial, gave us his unforgettable words, "Free at last! Free at last! Thank God Almighty, we are free at last." Let us join together and free ourselves from the shackles of archaic beliefs. We can then rejoice, "Home at last! Home at last! Thank God Almighty, we are Home at last."

MAPPING EXERCISE

1. This exercise will help you establish a Home Team. You can clarify your current level of support by examining your network of relationships, and those who frequent your inner circles.

Draw a large circle and then several concentric circles within. (See example)

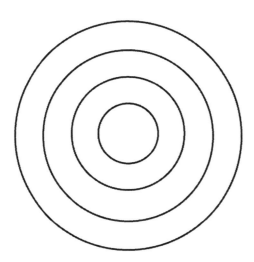

Place yourself in the center. Then place those closest to you in your inner circle. Work your way outward with friends and loved ones with whom you feel less close. Notice how many are in your inner circle. Do you feel comfortable sharing your True Self with them?

Are there any people within the inner circle who drain you or no longer serve you? What can you do to correct that? In the outer concentric rings are there others who might refuel you? What barriers can you remove to bring them closer? You can create a Home Team that nourishes and assists you. Membership is not static. Someone you meet today can join you on an important soulful expedition. If you lack a team, you can ask your GPS to help you find quality members. As a team, you expand each another. Your expansion accelerates your evolution and brings more beings of light into your life.

Begin to create a Home Team that sustains you. Identify a few people whom you would like to invite into your circles of influence. How could you approach them? The final step is to reach out and ask them to join your Home Team.

2. The final mapping exercise is an action plan to help you create inner peace and stay "At Home."

Action Plan
1) List the concrete steps you can take to:
   a. Strengthen your body
   b. Harmonize your emotions
   c. Renew your mind
   d. Open your heart
   e. Express your truth
   f. Live with purpose and vision
   g. Connect with Spirit
2) Which aspects of your life feel abundant? Which seem scarce? How can you expand your consciousness of prosperity?
3) How can you share this prosperity with others?
4) Set the intention to create a sacred time and space to stay "At Home" each day. How can you put this intention into practice?

5) Establish a back-up plan to return Home when you feel like an orphan.

6) What can you do to strengthen the heartbeat of connection?

7) List potential team members for your Home Team. How can you invite them? What can you offer? When will you contact them?

8) How do you want to celebrate your return? List the ways.

GUIDED VISUALIZATION

Imagine yourself being transported to a beautiful sanctuary in nature. It's exquisitely endowed with tropical vegetation, exotic animals, and fragrant, colorful flowers. The deep blue sky and healing yellow sun welcome you. A warm breeze caresses your cheeks. The sound of water in the distance beckons you.

You follow a path that leads to a holy grotto. It sparkles with light. Intricate crystal formations surround a clear pool of water. A steady stream falls from an overhanging rock, creating a gentle waterfall. A beautiful rhythm of water gurgles over the rocks. Ringlets form in the pool and extend outward.

You sit on the edge of a rock and dangle your feet in the cool water. You look down and see the reflection of your face. You smile at yourself. You reach down and cradle water in your palm. You sip the precious liquid. It quenches a deep thirst. The burdens of time fall from your body.

You look in the pool again. You see a young child, innocent with love. You giggle with delight. Abundance flows into your heart. Your senses become magnified. Everything you see, hear, feel, touch and taste is amplified – the gurgling water, the fresh air, the fragrant flowers. You sip the water once more. It cools and rejuvenates. A feeling of total bliss flows through your body. You inhale fresh air and know you are cared for and loved. All that you need is given you. You are conscious of the Divine Presence within and around you. You are eternally abundant. Love pours from your heart.

In the distance, you hear the sound of footsteps. Your friends and loved ones approach the grotto. Even those whom you once saw as enemies enter the sacred space. Everyone drinks from the pool. They transform into children. You recognize them as your brothers and sisters in Spirit. They recognize you. You share welcoming hugs and joyous laughter as you celebrate the return. Brilliant radiant lights surround the grotto and touch each child's heart. This marks the end, and the beginning, of your journey.

Embrace the moment. Splash with your loving friends in the holy water of life. Your heart pulsates with love and you happily share it with others. You are One in Spirit. You are Home at last!

EPILOGUE

ALL ROADS LEAD HOME

The wheel goes around, because the center is at rest.

– Old Quaker Proverb

New cell phones have a built-in GPS that monitors users wherever they go and locates destinations without a fuss. The accelerating speed of connectivity and the explosion of social networks on the Internet allow us to establish connection anywhere, anytime with practically anyone. The computer's capability for deciphering languages has begun to dissolve linguistic barriers, and, in the process, may allow us to become one world.

Global consciousness is shifting faster than the speed of the Internet. The worldwide web hurtles pictures and words for all to see. Thoughts precede materialization and generate sociological, spiritual, psychological, environmental, scientific and technological changes. This is already causing blessed unrest around the world.

Today, we face financial turbulence, climate change, world conflicts, and environmental disturbances. Though they create havoc, they also force us to face unexamined beliefs and behaviors. Increased consciousness cracks open the seed of illumination. Therein lies the sacred hope.

This hope empowers us to transform the globe. Rather than seeing Earth as a collection of separate nations, we can view ourselves in the diversity of faces and know that we are interconnected. We are the world. Thus united, we can heal the planet and sustain all. This was echoed in Barack Obama's June 4th, 2009 speech at the University of Cairo, Egypt when he told the assembly, "Our problems must be dealt with through partnership; our progress must be shared." He applauded the concept of *E pluribus unum* – out of many, one.

A collective one, connected with the Guiding Power of Spirit and acting with conscious intention, will accelerate the already quickening paradigm shift. The mass awakening of our species is birthing the spiritual human. Though we may embrace different faiths, we are participating in a universal experience. All roads lead Home.

Our awakening affects our families, neighborhoods, cities, states and nations. Together we can eradicate fear, heal wounds, and establish peace. This will hasten our evolution and bring forth incredible gifts of wisdom and manifestation.

It wasn't long ago, in the grand scheme of the universe, that our ancestors discovered the wheel. It is now time to spiral inward on the wheel of life and know that the kingdom is here, "on Earth as it is in heaven." All it requires is a commitment to step forward on this heroic adventure, Homeward bound.

I ask you to make that commitment. Remember the words of the anthropologist Margaret Mead, "Never doubt that a small group of thoughtful, committed citizens can change the world. Indeed, it is the only thing that ever has."

Together, arm in arm, heart-to-heart, we can walk and talk, speaking the blessing, *"May the Guiding Power of Spirit light the way and strengthen our bodies, harmonize our emotions, heal our minds, open our hearts, amplify our voices, and clarify our visions so that we resonate with love and become One."*

WELCOME HOME!

NOTES

Chapter One
1. Bloch, Douglas, *Words That Heal*, Bantam Books, New York, 1990, p. 104.
2. Holmes, Ernest, *This Thing Called You*, Tarcher/Penguin, New York, 1997, p. 31.
3. Thornton, James, *A Field Guide to the Soul: A Down-to-Earth Handbook of Spiritual Practice*, Bell Tower, New York, 1999, p. 41.
4. Lee, Ilchi, *Human Technology: A Toolkit for Authentic Living*, Healing Society, Sedona, 2005, p. 20.

Chapter Three
1. *Treatment of Birth Trauma in Infants and Children: Collected Works of William Emerson*, Ph.D., Vol. 1 - Emerson Training Seminars, Petaluma, CA, 1996.
2. Rowan, John, "The Trauma of Birth," *Primal Renaissance: The Journal of Primal Psychology*, Spring, 1996, Vol. 2, No.1, pp. 36.
3. Jacobson, Bertil, G. Eklund, L. Hamberger, D. Linnarsson, et al. "Perinatal Origin of Adult Self-destructive Behavior," *Acta Psychiatrica Scandinavica*, Vol. 76 (4), October, 1987, pp. 364-371.

Chapter Four
1. Linn, Denise, *The Secret Language of Signs*, Ballantine Books, New York, 1996. p. 6.
2. Hay, Louise, *You Can Heal Your Life*, Hay House, Carlsbad, 2004, p. 123.
3. Jung, C. G, *"Synchronicity: An Acausal Connecting Principle,"* Bollingen Foundation, Princeton, 1960. p. 25.
4. Randall, Bob, *Songman: The story of an Aboriginal Elder*, ABC Books, Sydney, 2003. p. 13.
5. "The Book of Genesis," Chapter 41, Verse 1-36.

Chapter Five
1. Tolle, Eckhart, *A New Earth: Awakening to Your Life's Purpose*, Plume, New York, 2006, p. 7.
2. Hanh, Thich Nhat, *Going Home: Jesus and Buddha as Brothers*, Riverhead Books, 1999, p. 18.

Chapter Six
1. Jackson, Phil and Hugh Delehanty, *Sacred Hoops: Spiritual Lessons of a Hardwood Warrior*, Hyperion, New York, 1995, p. 121.

Chapter Seven
1. Jampolsky, Jerry, *Love is Letting Go of Fear*, Celestial Arts, Berkeley, 1979. p. 17.
2. Maslow, Abraham, *Toward a Psychology of Being*, Wiley and Sons, New York, 1968. p. xvii.
3. Lee, Ilchi, *Brain Wave Vibration*, Best Life, Sedona, 2008, p. 22.
4. Holmes, Ernest, *How to Use the Science of Mind*, Dodd, Mead and Company, New York, 1950, pp. 2-3.
5. Buscaglia, Leo, *Loving Each Other: The Challenge for Human Relationships*, Slack, New York, 1984, p. 38.

Chapter Eight
1. Price, John Randolph, *The Abundance Book*, Hay House, Carlsbad, 1987, p. 32.
2. *A Course in Miracles*, Foundation for Inner Peace, Mill Valley, 2007, p. 152.
3. Hicks, Esther and Jerry, *Ask and It Is Given*, Hay House, Carlsbad, CA. 2004. p. 307.

Chapter Nine
1. Gaines, Edwene, *The Four Spiritual Laws of Prosperity*, Rodale, p. 45.
2. Hill, Napoleon, *Think and Grow Rich*, Wilshire Book Company, North Hollywood, 1966, p. 192.

BIBLIOGRAPHY

Albom, Mitch, *Tuesdays with Morrie: An Old Man, a Young Man, and Life's Greatest Lessons*, Doubleday, New York, 1997.

Bradshaw, John, *Homecoming: Reclaiming and Championing Your Inner Child*, Bantam Books, New York, 1980.

Bodian, Stephan, *Wake up Now: A Guide to the Journey of Spiritual Awakening*, McGraw Hill, New York, 2008.

Bloch, Douglas, *Words that Heal*, Bantam Books, New York, 1990.

Buscaglia, Leo, *Loving Each Other: The Challenge for Human Relationships*, Slack, New York, 1984.

Byrne, Rhonda, *The Secret*, Atria Books, 2006.

A Course in Miracles, Foundation for Inner Peace, Mill Valley, CA, 2007.

Casey, Karen, *Change Your Mind and Your Life Will Follow: 12 Simple Principles*, Conari Press, San Francisco, 2005.

Doidge, Norman, *The Brain that Changes Itself: Stories of Personal Triumph from the Frontiers of Brain Science*, Viking, New York, 2007.

Ford, Ariele, *The Soulmate Secret: Manifest the Love of Your Life with the Law of Attraction*, Harper One, New York, 2009.

Gaines, Edwene, *The Four Spiritual Laws of Prosperity*, Rodale, 2005.

Gayton, Richard, *The Forgiving Place: Choosing Peace After Violent Trauma*, Wellness Institute, Gretna, LA, 2001.

Goldberg, Dr. Philip, *Roadsigns: Navigating Your Path to Spiritual Happiness*, Rodale, 2003.

Hanh, Thich Nhat, *Going Home: Jesus and Buddha as Brothers*, Riverhead Books, 1999.

Hawkins, Dr. David, *The Eye of the I*, Veritas Publishing, Sedona, 2001.

——— Power *vs. Force: The Hidden Determinants of Human Behavior*, Hay House, Carlsbad, 2002.

Hay, Louise, *You Can Heal Your Life*, Hay House, Carlsbad, 2004.

Hendricks, Gay, *Conscious Breathing*, Bantam, New York, 1995.

————— *The Big Leap,* Harper One, New York, 2009.

Hendrix, Harville, *Keeping the Love You Find,* Atria Books, New York, 1992.

Hicks, Esther and Jerry, *Ask and It Is Given,* Hay House, Carlsbad, 2004.

Hill, Napoleon, *Think and Grow Rich,* Wilshire Book Company, North Hollywood, 1966.

Holmes, Ernest, *This Thing Called You,* Tarcher/Penguin, New York, 1997.

————— *How to Use the Science of Mind,* Dodd, Mead and Company, New York, 1950.

Houston, Jean, *The Possible Human: A Course in Enhancing Your Physical, Mental, and Creative Abilities,* Tarcher/Putnam, New York, 1982.

Jackson, Phil and Hugh Delehanty, *Sacred Hoops: Spiritual Lessons of a Hardwood Warrior,* Hyperion, New York, 1995.

Jampolsky, Jerry, *Love is Letting Go of Fear,* Celestial Arts, Berkeley, 1979.

Jampolsky, Jerry and Diane Cirincione, *Finding Our Way Home: Heartwarming Stories That Ignite Our Spiritual Core,* Hay House Carlsbad, 2008.

Jampolsky, Lee, *Walking Through Walls: Practical Spirituality for an Impractical World,* Celestial Arts, Berekley, 2005.

Judith, Anodea, *Wheels of Life: A User's Guide to the Chakra System,* Llewellyn Publications, St. Paul, MN, 2000.

Jung, C.G, "*Synchronicity: An Acausal Connecting Principle,*" Bollingen Foundation, Princeton, 1960.

Kabat-Zinn, Jon, *Coming to Our Senses: Healing Ourselves and the World Through Mindfulness,* Hyperion, New York, 2005.

Lee, Ilchi, *Brain Wave Vibration,* Best Life, Sedona, 2008.

————— *Human Technology: A Toolkit for Authentic Living,* Healing Society, Sedona, 2005.

Linn, Denise, *The Secret Language of Signs,* Ballantine Books, New York, 1996.

Maslow, Abraham, *The Farthest Reaches of Human Nature,* Penguin, New York, 1976.

Maslow, Abraham, *Toward a Psychology of Being,* Wiley and Sons, New York, 1968.

Miller, Ann, *The Secret to Abundance Consciousness: Breaking Free from the Fears That Bind You*, OPA, Chandler, AZ, 2005.

Moore, Kirk, *Tara's Angels: One Family's Extraordinary Journey of Courage and Healing*, Opa Publishing, Irvine, CA, 2003.

Moss, Robert, *Dreaming True: How to Dream Your Future and Change Your Life for the Better*, Pocket Books, New York, 2000.

Mundy, Dr. Jon, *What is Mysticism*, Royal Fireworks Press, Unionville, New York, 2008.

Nichols, Lisa, *No Matter What: 9 Steps to Living the Life You Love*, Wellness Central, New York, 2009.

Price, John Randolph, *The Abundance Book*, Hay House, Carlsbad, 1987.

Randall, Bob, *Songman: The Story of an Aboriginal Elder*, ABC Books, Sydney, 2003.

Renard, Gary, *Your Immortal Reality: How to Break the Cycle of Birth and Death*, Hay House, Carlsbad, 2006.

Riso, Don and Russ Hudson, *The Wisdom of the Enneagram: The Complete Guide to Psychological and Spiritual Growth for the Nine Personality Types*, Bantam, New York, 1999.

Spieker, Michelle Morris, *The Cherished Self: How to Give Back to Yourself When You're Living a Life That Takes All You've Got*, Quality Books, 2000.

Tetteh, Bro. Ishmael, *Soul Processing: The Path to Freedom*, Asante and Hittscher, Ghana, 2002.

Thornton, James, *A Field Guide to the Soul: A Down-to-Earth Handbook of Spiritual Practice*, Bell Tower, New York, 1999.

Tolle, Eckhart, A *New Earth: Awakening to Your Life's Purpose*, Plume, 2005.

———— *The Power of Now: A Guide to Spiritual Enlightenment*, New World Library, Novato, Canada, 1999.

Williamson, Marianne, *Everyday Grace: Having Hope, Finding Forgiveness and Making Miracles*, Riverhead books, New York, 2002.

———— *A Return to Love*, Harper Collins, New York, 1992.

Wolinsky, Stephen, *The Dark Side of the Inner Child*, Bramble Books, Norfolk, CO, 1993.

Zimberoff, Diane, *Longing for Belonging: Pilgrimage of Transformation*, Wellness Press, Issaquah, WA, 2008.

ABOUT THE AUTHOR

Leonard Szymczak, MSW, LCSW, has been a psychotherapist and educator for over 35 years, both in Australia and America, working with individuals, couples, families and groups. He was Director of the Family Therapy Program at the Marriage and Family Centre in Sydney, Australia and later served as a senior affiliate therapist with the Family Institute at Northwestern University. A licensed clinical social worker, Leonard has conducted countless seminars and has written numerous articles on mental health, personal growth, stress management, and relationship building. He is the author of the novel *Cuckoo Forevermore*, a satire on psychotherapy, and its sequel, *Kookaburra's Last Laugh*, due out in 2010.

Throughout his life, Leonard has been committed to ongoing personal growth and believes firmly in the power of the individual to overcome adversity and transform one's life. Like the mythologist Joseph Campbell, he utilizes the concept of the hero's journey to help individuals reshape their stories into amazing adventures. He firmly believes that when connected to the Guiding Power of Spirit, individuals can shift problems and pain into opportunities for healing and growth and return Home to love and inner peace.

Leonard lives near the beach in Southern California where he writes, conducts seminars, and maintains a private practice. He is the proud father of two adult children.

www.leonardszymczak.com

Please share your personal stories about your internal GPS and the journey Home to inner peace.

I invite you to visit **www.theroadmaphome.com** and share any personal stories where your GPS has guided you through life or you have experienced Home. Your message can inspire others to realize that they are not alone and that they can connect with the Guiding Power of Spirit to heal their lives and guide them Home to love and inner peace.

For more information about Leonard's seminars, speaking engagements, products, or free downloads, or if you would like to contact Leonard, visit him at:

www.leonardszymczak.com
email: leonard@leonardszymczak.com

Festival

You

4385317

Made in the USA
Charleston, SC
12 January 2010